Copyright © 2023 by Connor A. Anderson (Author)

All rights reserved. No part of this book may be reproduced or utilized in any form or by any means, electronic or mechanical, including photocopying, recording or by any information storage and retrieval system, without permission in writing from the publisher, except for brief quotations in critical articles or reviews.

The content of this book is based on various sources and is intended for educational and entertainment purposes only. While the author has made every effort to ensure the accuracy, completeness, and reliability of the information provided, the information may be subject to errors, omissions, or inaccuracies. Therefore, the author makes no warranties, express or implied, regarding the content of this book.

Readers are advised to seek the guidance of a licensed professional before attempting any techniques or actions outlined in this book. The author is not responsible for any losses, damages, or injuries that may arise from the use of information contained within. The information provided in this book is not intended to be a substitute for professional advice, and readers should not rely solely on the information presented.

By reading this book, readers acknowledge that the author is not providing legal, financial, medical, or professional advice. Any reliance on the information contained in this book is solely at the reader's own risk.

Thank you for selecting this book as a valuable source of knowledge and inspiration. Our aim is to provide you with insights and information that will enrich your understanding and enhance your personal growth. We appreciate your decision to embark on this journey of discovery with us, and we hope that this book will exceed your expectations and leave a lasting impact on your life.

Title: Origins and Ancient Games
Subtitle: Unveiling the Ancient Battlegrounds of Athleticism

Series: Sports Through Time: A Comprehensive History
Author: Connor A. Anderson

Table of Contents

Introduction 5
The allure of ancient sports 5
Significance of understanding origins 9
Link between ancient games and modern sports 13

Chapter 1: The Cradle of Competition 17
Early human athleticism 17
Sports in prehistoric cultures 21
Role of physical prowess in survival 26

Chapter 2: Ancient Mesopotamia and Beyond 31
Early records of sports in Mesopotamia 31
Ancient ball games and their rituals 36
Sporting events in early civilizations 41

Chapter 3: Athleticism in Ancient Egypt 46
Sporting Activities in Ancient Egyptian Society 46
Sporting events as religious ceremonies 51
Hieroglyphics depicting ancient games 56

Chapter 4: Ancient Greek Panhellenic Games 60
The significance of the Olympic Games 60
Athleticism as an embodiment of Greek values 66
Origins of various Greek sports and their rules 72

Chapter 5: The Roman Arena and Beyond 78
Gladiatorial contests and chariot races 78
Roman influence on sports culture 83

Spread of Roman-style amphitheaters and games 89

Chapter 6: Indigenous Sports and Ancient Americas 94

Sports in Native American societies 94

Ball games of Mesoamerica and South America 100

Cultural and spiritual dimensions of indigenous sports .. 105

Chapter 7: Sporting Traditions of the Far East 110

Ancient Chinese martial arts and competitions 110

Martial arts in Japanese culture 116

Early forms of archery, wrestling, and more 121

Conclusion 127

The lasting legacy of ancient sports 127

Lessons from ancient athletic ideals 132

How ancient sports paved the way for modern competitions 137

Wordbook 142

Supplementary Materials 145

Introduction
The allure of ancient sports

Sports have always held a special place in human society. From the thrill of competition to the camaraderie among athletes and spectators, the world of sports has a unique ability to capture our imagination and stir our passions. But what is it about ancient sports, those long-forgotten contests of strength and skill, that continues to captivate our hearts and minds? In this section, we delve into the enduring allure of ancient sports, seeking to understand why these games, rituals, and feats of athleticism continue to resonate with us today.

A Glimpse into the Past

Imagine standing on the dusty plains of ancient Greece, surrounded by thousands of cheering spectators, as athletes from all corners of the Greek world prepare to compete in the Olympic Games. Picture yourself in the grand colosseums of Rome, where gladiators faced off in life-and-death battles for the entertainment of the masses. These scenes, though from distant epochs, have a timeless quality that draws us in. They offer a glimpse into the lives and passions of our ancestors, reminding us that the human spirit has always sought challenges, tests of skill, and the thrill of victory.

The Universality of Competition

One of the most intriguing aspects of ancient sports is their universality. Sports, in some form, have been a part of nearly every human culture throughout history. Whether it was the ball games of Mesoamerica, the martial arts of ancient China, or the chariot races of Rome, societies around the world have developed their own unique sporting traditions. These ancient sports were not just about physical prowess; they embodied the values, beliefs, and aspirations of their respective cultures.

The Physical and Spiritual Connection

Ancient sports were often deeply intertwined with the physical and spiritual aspects of life. In ancient Egypt, sporting events were considered religious ceremonies, with athletic prowess seen as a divine gift. Hieroglyphics and artwork depict these events, serving as a testament to their significance. The Greeks believed that the body and mind were interconnected, and the pursuit of physical excellence was as important as intellectual pursuits. This holistic view of the athlete as a well-rounded individual continues to influence modern sports.

Lessons from the Past

As we explore the allure of ancient sports, we find that they offer valuable lessons for our contemporary world. The dedication, discipline, and determination exhibited by ancient athletes are qualities that resonate with us today. Their pursuit of excellence, their drive to push the limits of human ability, and their unwavering commitment to their craft inspire us to strive for greatness in our own lives.

Bridging the Gap to Modern Sports

Ancient sports serve as a bridge between the past and the present. By studying the games and athletic ideals of our ancestors, we gain insight into the origins of the sports we love today. We see how the values and traditions of ancient sports have shaped the sporting culture of our modern world. From the Olympic Games of antiquity to the global sporting spectacles of the 21st century, there is a clear lineage that connects the two.

In the chapters that follow, we will embark on a journey through time and across cultures, exploring the origins of sports in ancient civilizations and the enduring legacy they have left behind. We will delve into the physical and philosophical aspects of ancient sports, uncovering the stories of legendary athletes and the lessons they offer. Through this exploration, we hope to not only satisfy your curiosity about the past but also inspire you to see the world of sports in a new and profound light.

So, join us as we step into the arena of history, where ancient sports come to life, and the allure of competition beckons us to discover the roots of our shared sporting heritage.

Significance of understanding origins

In the world of sports, as in many aspects of life, knowing where we come from provides invaluable insights into who we are and where we're headed. This is especially true when it comes to the history of sports. To fully appreciate the significance of ancient sports and their impact on modern society, it's essential to understand their origins. In this section, we explore why delving into the origins of sports is not just a historical exercise but a journey of discovery that enriches our understanding of human culture, society, and ourselves.

A Tapestry of Human History

Sports are not isolated phenomena but are interwoven into the tapestry of human history. The development and evolution of sports mirror the broader trends, innovations, and challenges that societies have faced over millennia. By studying the origins of sports, we gain a deeper appreciation for the complex interplay of culture, politics, religion, and technology that has shaped our world.

Roots of Identity and Tradition

Understanding the origins of sports is akin to exploring the roots of our cultural identity. Many modern sports have deep historical ties to specific regions, communities, or peoples. For example, the ancient Olympic

Games were a quintessential expression of Greek culture, and their revival in the modern era carries on that tradition. When we embrace these origins, we connect with the traditions and values that have been passed down through generations.

Unearthing Human Ingenuity

The evolution of sports is a testament to human ingenuity. From the early games of ancient Mesopotamia to the intricate martial arts of the Far East, our ancestors displayed remarkable creativity and resourcefulness in developing sports and athletic competitions. By uncovering the origins of these sports, we celebrate the inventive spirit that has driven human progress.

Lessons from the Past

The past is a repository of valuable lessons. When we delve into the origins of sports, we encounter the stories of athletes who faced adversity, overcame challenges, and achieved greatness. These stories inspire us to strive for excellence in our own pursuits, both on and off the field. The ancient ideals of sportsmanship, fair play, and dedication remain as relevant today as they were centuries ago.

Contextualizing Modern Sports

To truly appreciate the sports we love today, we must understand their historical context. The evolution of rules, equipment, and even the reasons for competition shed light on how our favorite sports have developed. It allows us to see how they have adapted to changing times and how they continue to reflect the values and aspirations of our society.

Preserving Cultural Heritage

The study of ancient sports plays a crucial role in preserving cultural heritage. Many indigenous sports and traditional games are at risk of being lost to time. By documenting their origins and significance, we ensure that these rich cultural traditions are passed on to future generations.

Fostering a Global Perspective

Finally, the exploration of sports origins fosters a global perspective. Sports have transcended borders and brought people from diverse backgrounds together. By understanding the origins of sports in different regions and cultures, we gain a deeper appreciation for the common threads that bind us as a global community.

In the pages that follow, we will embark on a journey through time and across continents, tracing the origins of various sports in ancient civilizations. We will uncover the stories of athletes, examine the rituals and ceremonies surrounding sports, and explore the profound impact of sports on society. Together, we will discover that the roots of our favorite pastimes run deep, and by understanding these origins, we gain a richer appreciation for the enduring allure of sports.

So, join us as we dive into the annals of history, where the significance of understanding origins becomes clear, and the story of sports unfolds in all its complexity and splendor.

Link between ancient games and modern sports

As we embark on this journey through the annals of history and explore the allure and significance of ancient sports, it becomes abundantly clear that the past is not a distant realm separate from our contemporary world. Instead, it is intricately woven into the fabric of our modern sports culture. In this section, we will unravel the threads that connect the ancient games of yesteryears to the sports we know and love today, demonstrating that the echoes of antiquity resonate in every stadium, arena, and playing field.

A Legacy of Competition

Competition is the beating heart of sports, and its roots stretch deep into the past. Ancient civilizations understood the primal urge to test one's mettle against others, and they created games and contests that served as precursors to the organized sports we have today. The drive to win, the thrill of victory, and the lessons learned in defeat have been constants throughout history.

Athletic Prowess and Physical Excellence

The pursuit of physical excellence has always been a core principle of sports. In the ancient world, athletes trained rigorously to develop their strength, speed, and agility. The Greeks, in particular, celebrated the ideal of the well-rounded athlete, and their emphasis on physical fitness and prowess has left an indelible mark on modern sports training and conditioning.

The Olympic Ideal

The ancient Olympic Games, held in Olympia, Greece, were a pinnacle of athletic achievement. They served as a platform for the world's best athletes to compete and demonstrate their prowess. The revival of the modern Olympic Games in the late 19th century was a deliberate homage to this ancient tradition. Today, the Olympic Games remain a global celebration of unity, competition, and excellence, embodying the same ideals that inspired their ancient counterparts.

Rules and Regulations

Ancient sports were not merely displays of physical prowess; they were governed by rules and regulations that ensured fair play and a level playing field. The concept of rules in sports has endured through the ages, evolving and adapting to the changing nature of competition. Understanding the origins of these rules helps us appreciate the importance of fairness and sportsmanship in contemporary sports.

Sporting Equipment and Technology

The evolution of sports equipment and technology is another area where ancient influences are evident. From the development of rudimentary sporting implements in ancient times to the cutting-edge equipment used by athletes today, there is a clear line of innovation and progress. Ancient innovations, such as the introduction of the discus or the chariot wheel, laid the groundwork for the sophisticated gear of modern sports.

Spectatorship and Entertainment

The ancient world was no stranger to the excitement of sports events. The grand stadiums of Rome, the amphitheaters of Greece, and the ball courts of Mesoamerica were hubs of entertainment and communal bonding. These ancient venues set the stage for the modern sports arenas and stadiums where millions of fans gather to cheer for their favorite teams and athletes.

Cultural and Spiritual Significance

Ancient sports often had deep cultural and spiritual significance. They were not merely contests of physical skill but were imbued with meaning and symbolism. This aspect of ancient sports has carried over into modern times, where sporting events can serve as platforms for cultural expression, national pride, and even moments of unity and reflection.

The Continuity of Human Spirit

Perhaps the most profound link between ancient games and modern sports is the continuity of the human spirit. The same passion, determination, and indomitable will that drove athletes in ancient times continue to fuel the athletes of today. Whether it's a sprinter striving to break a world record or a team battling for a championship, the essence of competition remains unchanged.

In the chapters that follow, we will delve deeper into the origins of specific sports in ancient civilizations, tracing their evolution and the enduring legacy they have left behind. We will uncover the stories of legendary athletes, explore the rituals and ceremonies surrounding sports, and examine the profound impact of sports on society. Through this exploration, we will gain a deeper understanding of how the ancient games of our forebears continue to shape and inspire the sports culture of our modern world.

So, join us as we bridge the gap between ancient games and modern sports, where the past informs the present, and the spirit of competition transcends the ages.

Chapter 1: The Cradle of Competition
Early human athleticism

The story of sports begins long before the grand arenas and organized competitions of ancient civilizations. It begins with the very essence of human nature—the innate drive to move, compete, and excel. Early human athleticism was an unscripted, primal form of physical activity, born out of necessity and honed through survival. In this section, we embark on a journey back in time to witness the origins of human athleticism, a journey that takes us to the dawn of our species.

The Hunter-Gatherer Athletic Ideal

Our prehistoric ancestors, the hunter-gatherers, lived in a world where physical prowess was a matter of life and death. Survival depended on their ability to run, jump, climb, and throw with precision. While they may not have called it "sports" in the way we do today, their daily activities were exercises in athleticism.

Running the Gauntlet of the Savanna

Imagine early humans on the African savanna, stalking prey or evading predators. Their endurance and speed were finely tuned instruments of survival. The ability to sprint short distances, maintain a steady jog for extended periods, or track game over long distances were essential skills.

The Vertical Challenge

Early humans also had to master the art of climbing. Trees provided both refuge and sustenance, and the ability to ascend with agility was crucial. This natural athleticism laid the groundwork for climbing sports and activities we see today.

Throwing and Accuracy

The ability to throw objects with precision was another vital skill. Whether it was a spear aimed at prey or a rock used for self-defense, early humans developed remarkable accuracy in their throws. This innate athleticism would eventually give rise to sports like javelin throwing and archery.

Rituals of Strength and Endurance

Early human societies often incorporated physical contests and rituals into their cultures. These rituals served not only as a form of entertainment but also as a means of establishing hierarchies and resolving conflicts.

Test of Strength

Competitions of strength were common, with individuals showcasing their physical prowess through challenges like lifting heavy objects, wrestling, or tests of endurance. These contests were precursors to modern weightlifting and combat sports.

Endurance Challenges

Endurance was highly valued, and individuals would engage in long-distance runs or endurance tests that pushed the limits of their physical abilities. These challenges laid the foundation for modern marathon races and ultramarathons.

The Evolutionary Advantage

The development of athleticism in early humans wasn't just a matter of survival; it was also a key factor in our species' evolutionary success. Physical fitness conferred advantages in hunting, foraging, and protection from predators. It was a means of ensuring the survival and well-being of the tribe.

Lessons from Our Ancestors

As we look back at the athleticism of our early human ancestors, we find valuable lessons that resonate with us today. The importance of a well-rounded set of physical skills, the significance of endurance, and the innate drive to compete and improve are all traits that continue to define modern sports and athletes.

In the chapters that follow, we will delve deeper into the ancient sports and competitions of various cultures, tracing their evolution and the enduring legacy they have left behind. We will uncover the stories of legendary athletes, explore the rituals and ceremonies surrounding sports, and examine the profound impact of sports on society. Through this exploration, we will gain a deeper understanding of how the athleticism of our earliest ancestors laid the foundation for the organized sports and competitions we know today.

So, join us as we journey into the cradle of competition, where the raw athleticism of early humans shaped the course of sports history, and the spirit of competition burned brightly in the hearts of our forebears.

Sports in prehistoric cultures

In the dim recesses of prehistory, long before the grand stadiums and formalized rules of modern sports, our ancestors were already engaging in activities that bore the hallmarks of competition and athleticism. These early forms of sports-like endeavors were not only a reflection of the human desire for physical expression but also a means of social bonding, skill development, and cultural expression. In this section, we will journey back in time to explore the sports and games of prehistoric cultures, where the seeds of organized competition were sown.

The Primordial Playground

Prehistoric humans inhabited a world fraught with challenges, where survival depended on physical prowess and adaptability. In this harsh environment, physical activities that mimicked the skills needed for survival naturally evolved into games and sports.

Primitive Ball Games

One of the earliest forms of organized physical activity was the use of balls made from materials like animal bladders or plant fibers. Early humans likely engaged in games of catch or contests to see who could propel these primitive balls the farthest. These rudimentary ball games planted the seeds for sports like soccer, basketball, and volleyball.

Racing and Chasing

Chasing and racing were essential skills for both hunters and prey. Early humans may have engaged in foot races, sometimes as part of rituals or competitions. These races were the precursors to modern track and field events.

Rituals and Ceremonies

Prehistoric cultures often incorporated physical contests into their rituals and ceremonies. These contests served as a means of connecting with the spiritual world, resolving disputes, and affirming social hierarchies.

Ritual Combat

Ritual combat, often referred to as "combat sports" in the context of prehistoric cultures, was a common form of expression. These contests were not necessarily about causing harm but rather about demonstrating prowess and resolve. They were forerunners to modern martial arts.

Ceremonial Races

Some prehistoric cultures held races as part of their religious ceremonies. These races symbolized the journey of the soul or served as offerings to deities. The spiritual significance of these races can still be seen in modern religious festivals and processions.

Artifacts and Artistry

The material remnants of prehistoric sports and games can be found in the archaeological record. These artifacts and depictions offer a window into the past and provide clues about the significance of these activities.

Ancient Sporting Implements

Archaeological finds, such as primitive sports equipment and gaming pieces, reveal the importance of these activities in prehistoric cultures. These artifacts often show signs of wear and tear, suggesting they were used frequently and with enthusiasm.

Cave Paintings and Petroglyphs

Cave paintings and petroglyphs found in various parts of the world depict scenes of hunting, racing, and athletic contests. These ancient artworks provide insights into the role of sports in the cultural and social life of prehistoric societies.

Cultural Significance

Sports-like activities in prehistoric cultures weren't just physical pastimes; they were deeply embedded in the fabric of society. They served as a means of socialization, skill development, and cultural expression.

Community Bonding

Engaging in sports-like activities allowed members of prehistoric communities to bond and build social cohesion. These activities helped establish trust, cooperation, and a sense of belonging among individuals.

Skill Acquisition

Many prehistoric sports and games had practical applications. They helped individuals acquire essential skills for survival, such as agility, coordination, and teamwork. These skills were then passed down through generations.

Lessons from the Past

As we delve into the sports and games of prehistoric cultures, we find valuable lessons that still resonate today. The universality of sports as a means of physical expression and social bonding transcends time and culture. The games and activities of our ancestors provide a testament to the enduring appeal of competition and athleticism.

In the chapters that follow, we will continue our exploration of the ancient sports of different cultures and time periods, tracing their evolution and the profound impact they have had on modern sports. We will uncover the stories of legendary athletes, delve into the rituals and ceremonies surrounding sports, and examine how these activities have shaped society and human culture throughout history.

So, join us as we journey further into the cradle of competition, where the ancient sports and games of prehistoric cultures reveal the deep-seated human desire for physical expression, camaraderie, and the thrill of competition.

Role of physical prowess in survival

In the ancient world, long before the emergence of complex societies and the advent of organized sports, physical prowess was a fundamental attribute that determined the fate of individuals and their communities. Survival hinged on one's ability to adapt, to thrive in a challenging environment, and to overcome obstacles both natural and man-made. In this section, we delve into the profound role that physical prowess played in the survival of early humans, and how this primal need laid the foundation for the development of athleticism and sports.

The Challenge of Survival

Life in the prehistoric world was fraught with dangers. Early humans faced not only the harsh elements but also formidable predators and the constant struggle for food and shelter. In this environment, physical prowess was not a luxury but a necessity for survival.

The Hunt for Sustenance

Hunting was a vital aspect of early human existence. The ability to track, capture, and kill game was the difference between a full belly and starvation. Early hunters needed strength, agility, and endurance to chase down their prey, skills that are echoed in modern sports like sprinting and long-distance running.

Defending Against Predators

Early humans were not always at the top of the food chain. They had to defend themselves and their communities against formidable predators. Physical prowess, including the ability to fight, run, and climb, was essential for survival.

Adaptation and Innovation

Physical prowess wasn't just about brute strength; it was also about adaptability and innovation. Early humans had to adapt to a wide range of environments, from dense forests to open savannas, and devise creative solutions to the challenges they encountered.

Tools and Weapons

The development of tools and weapons was a significant leap in the evolution of early humans. It allowed them to extend their physical capabilities, enhancing their ability to hunt, protect themselves, and build shelter. The creation of tools and the skills required to use them paved the way for modern sports equipment and technology.

Agility and Coordination

Early humans developed agility and coordination through activities like climbing trees, navigating rough terrain, and crossing bodies of water. These skills were crucial for avoiding danger and accessing new sources of food and shelter.

Social Hierarchies and Cooperation

Physical prowess wasn't only about individual survival; it also played a role in establishing social hierarchies and fostering cooperation within early human communities.

Leadership and Respect

Individuals who demonstrated exceptional physical abilities often earned the respect and admiration of their peers. They were looked up to as leaders and protectors within their communities.

Teamwork and Cooperation

Many survival challenges required teamwork and cooperation. Whether it was a group of hunters working together to take down a large animal or a community coming together to build a shelter, physical prowess and coordination were vital for collective success.

The Primal Drive to Compete

The drive to compete and excel is deeply rooted in human nature. Early humans competed not just for survival but also for status and recognition within their communities.

Friendly Challenges

Friendly competitions and challenges were common among early humans. These contests allowed individuals to showcase their physical abilities, test their limits, and earn the admiration of their peers.

Spurring Progress

Competition among early humans also served as a catalyst for progress. It pushed individuals to develop new skills, discover innovative solutions to problems, and continuously improve their physical abilities.

Lessons from the Past

The role of physical prowess in survival teaches us that the human body is a remarkable instrument of adaptation and innovation. The skills and attributes that early humans honed in the crucible of survival are the same qualities that continue to define athletes and sports today.

In the chapters that follow, we will explore how the primal need for physical prowess shaped the development of organized sports in ancient civilizations. We will uncover the stories of legendary athletes, examine the rituals and ceremonies surrounding sports, and delve into the profound impact of sports on society. Through this exploration, we will gain a deeper understanding of how the roots of athleticism and competition trace back to the very essence of human survival.

So, join us as we journey further into the cradle of competition, where the role of physical prowess in survival becomes a testament to the enduring human spirit and the timeless appeal of sports.

Chapter 2: Ancient Mesopotamia and Beyond
Early records of sports in Mesopotamia

Mesopotamia, often referred to as the "cradle of civilization," was home to one of the world's earliest and most influential cultures. This ancient land, located between the Tigris and Euphrates rivers, gave birth to remarkable achievements in agriculture, architecture, and governance. But beyond these accomplishments, Mesopotamia also had a rich sporting tradition that left behind valuable records, providing us with a glimpse into the sports and athletic activities of this early civilization.

The Birthplace of Writing

One of the most significant contributions of Mesopotamia to human history was the development of writing. The Sumerians, who inhabited this region around 3500 BCE, created one of the world's first writing systems known as cuneiform. This remarkable invention allowed them to document various aspects of their society, including sports and games.

Cuneiform Tablets

Cuneiform tablets, made from clay and impressed with wedge-shaped markings, have provided valuable insights into the daily lives of the Sumerians. Among these records are accounts of sporting events, contests, and physical activities that were an integral part of their culture.

Sporting Events in Mesopotamia

Sports and athletic competitions in Mesopotamia were not just recreational activities; they were deeply ingrained in the social, religious, and even political aspects of society. The early records reveal a diverse range of sports and sporting events that captivated the hearts and minds of the ancient Mesopotamians.

Foot Races

Foot races were a popular form of competition in Mesopotamia. Runners would compete in races of various distances, often in front of large crowds. These events were not only a test of speed but also served as opportunities for individuals to gain recognition and honor within their communities.

Wrestling

Wrestling was another prominent sport, and it was often depicted in Mesopotamian art and literature. Wrestlers engaged in fierce contests of strength and technique, with the victors earning acclaim and prestige.

Archery and Spear Throwing

Archery and spear throwing were essential skills for hunting and warfare in ancient Mesopotamia. These skills were honed through sporting contests that challenged individuals to showcase their accuracy and precision. Archers and spear throwers were celebrated for their ability to hit targets with remarkable skill.

Ball Games

Ball games played with a leather ball filled with air were also popular in Mesopotamia. These games were both recreational and competitive, with players using their hands or other body parts to keep the ball in motion. The ancient origins of ball games in Mesopotamia can be seen as precursors to modern sports like soccer and basketball.

Religious Significance

Sports in Mesopotamia often held religious significance. Many sporting events were conducted as part of religious ceremonies and festivals, with the aim of pleasing the gods and ensuring favorable outcomes for the community.

Ritualistic Races

Foot races and other physical contests were incorporated into religious rituals. These races symbolized the struggle between gods and demons or the journey of the soul in the afterlife. Winning such races was not only a matter of personal pride but also a way of honoring the divine.

Offerings to Deities

Some sporting events involved offerings to deities. Competitions were held to determine who would have the honor of presenting offerings to gods and goddesses. These contests underscored the belief that physical prowess was a form of divine favor.

Records of Sport and Leisure

While many early records focused on the formal aspects of sports and competitions, some also provide glimpses into the leisure activities of the Mesopotamians. These records show that sports and games were not limited to grand events but were also enjoyed in more informal settings.

Board Games

Board games such as the Royal Game of Ur were popular pastimes. These games required strategy and skill and provided entertainment in homes and social gatherings.

Music and Dance

Music and dance were often intertwined with sporting events and festivals. Drums, flutes, and other musical instruments accompanied athletic competitions and added to the festive atmosphere.

Lessons from Ancient Mesopotamia

The early records of sports in Mesopotamia offer valuable lessons about the enduring appeal of physical activity and competition. They remind us that sports have always been an integral part of human culture, serving not only as a source of entertainment but also as a means of social bonding, religious expression, and personal development.

In the chapters that follow, we will continue to explore the sporting traditions of ancient civilizations and their impact on the development of modern sports. We will uncover the stories of legendary athletes, examine the rituals and ceremonies surrounding sports, and delve into the profound influence of sports on society. Through this exploration, we will gain a deeper understanding of how the ancient sporting heritage of Mesopotamia has left an indelible mark on the sporting culture of our modern world.

So, join us as we journey further into the world of ancient sports, where the early records of Mesopotamia illuminate the rich tapestry of human athleticism and competition.

Ancient ball games and their rituals

Ball games have been a source of entertainment and competition in societies throughout history, and ancient Mesopotamia was no exception. In this section, we delve into the world of ancient ball games that were played in the heart of civilization. These games were more than just pastimes; they were deeply rooted in the culture and rituals of the time.

The Appeal of Ball Games

Ball games have an innate appeal that transcends time and place. The simplicity of a ball and the potential for creative play make them accessible to people of all ages and backgrounds. In ancient Mesopotamia, these games were not only a form of recreation but also a means of celebrating life, honoring deities, and fostering social bonds.

The Oldest Ball Game

Among the various ball games played in ancient Mesopotamia, one of the most well-documented is the game known as "Tsu-chu" or "Cuju." This game dates back over two thousand years and is considered one of the oldest forms of soccer.

The Rules of Cuju

Cuju was played with a leather ball stuffed with feathers or hair. The goal of the game was to kick the ball through a small opening in a net or between two bamboo poles. While the basic objective of scoring goals remains a fundamental aspect of modern soccer, Cuju had its own unique rules and traditions.

Rituals and Symbolism

Cuju was not just a sport; it was a ritualistic activity with deep symbolic significance. The game was often played as part of religious ceremonies, agricultural festivals, or to celebrate important occasions. Participants believed that the act of kicking the ball symbolically expelled negative energies and brought good fortune.

Social and Cultural Significance

Ancient ball games in Mesopotamia were not limited to Cuju. Various forms of ball games were played in different contexts, each with its own cultural and social significance.

Community Bonding

Ball games served as a means of social bonding. Communities would come together to play, fostering a sense of unity and camaraderie. These games helped strengthen social ties and provided a break from the rigors of daily life.

Ritual Contests

Some ball games in Mesopotamia were contests between rival groups or individuals. These contests often had religious or political implications and were used to settle disputes or establish hierarchies. The winners of such contests were celebrated and honored.

Records and Depictions

The knowledge of ancient ball games in Mesopotamia comes from a variety of sources, including cuneiform tablets, artworks, and inscriptions. These records offer glimpses into how these games were played, their rules, and their cultural significance.

Cuneiform Texts

Cuneiform tablets from Mesopotamia contain references to ball games, including Cuju. These texts provide insights into the rules of the game, its participants, and the contexts in which it was played.

Artistic Representations

Ancient artworks often depict scenes of ball games. These depictions show players engaged in spirited competition, providing visual evidence of the popularity and cultural significance of these games.

Legacy and Influence

The legacy of ancient ball games in Mesopotamia can be seen in the enduring popularity of modern sports like soccer, basketball, and volleyball. The basic concept of kicking or propelling a ball into a target or opposing team's goal is a testament to the timelessness of these activities.

The Global Reach of Soccer

Soccer, in particular, has grown to become the world's most popular sport, with millions of enthusiasts across the globe. The roots of this beloved sport can be traced back to the ancient ball games played in the heart of Mesopotamia.

Lessons from Ancient Ball Games

The ball games of ancient Mesopotamia remind us that the appeal of sports goes far beyond mere competition. These games were woven into the fabric of society, serving as instruments of celebration, bonding, and cultural expression. They were a testament to the universal human desire for play, recreation, and connection.

In the chapters that follow, we will continue our exploration of the sporting traditions of ancient civilizations and their influence on the development of modern sports. We will uncover the stories of legendary athletes, examine the rituals and ceremonies surrounding sports, and delve into the profound impact of sports on society. Through this exploration, we will gain a deeper understanding of how the games and rituals of ancient ball sports in Mesopotamia continue to resonate in the world of sports today.

So, join us as we journey further into the realm of ancient ball games, where the simple act of kicking a ball symbolized much more than a game—it represented a celebration of life, a connection to the divine, and a testament to the enduring spirit of play.

Sporting events in early civilizations

Early civilizations, from Mesopotamia to Egypt, Greece, and Rome, celebrated the spirit of competition and physical prowess through a rich tapestry of sporting events. These events were not merely forms of entertainment but integral aspects of society, deeply intertwined with culture, religion, and governance. In this section, we explore the diverse array of sporting events that flourished in the cradle of civilization and beyond.

The Cradle of Sporting Traditions

Early civilizations, marked by their impressive achievements in agriculture, architecture, and governance, also possessed a vibrant sporting culture. Sporting events were more than just displays of physical prowess; they were opportunities for communities to come together, celebrate their heritage, and showcase the skills and talents of their citizens.

The Panhellenic Games

In ancient Greece, the Panhellenic Games, including the Olympic Games, Pythian Games, Nemean Games, and Isthmian Games, were among the most prestigious and celebrated sporting events. These competitions brought together athletes from different city-states to compete in a wide range of athletic disciplines, from foot races to combat sports.

The Circus Maximus

In ancient Rome, the Circus Maximus was a massive chariot racing arena that could accommodate over 150,000 spectators. Chariot racing was a beloved sport that captivated the Roman populace, and races in the Circus Maximus were some of the most popular events in the city.

Beyond Greece and Rome

While Greece and Rome are often celebrated for their sporting traditions, they were not the only early civilizations to embrace competitive events. Other cultures around the world also had their own unique sporting traditions that reflected their values, beliefs, and societal structures.

Ancient Egypt

In ancient Egypt, sports and physical activities held cultural and religious significance. Activities like wrestling, archery, and swimming were not only recreational but also featured in religious rituals and ceremonies. The ancient Egyptians celebrated the Nile Festival, which included swimming races and boat competitions.

Mesoamerican Ballgames

The Mesoamerican ballgames, played by civilizations such as the Maya and Aztec, were unique and highly ritualized. These ballgames involved teams trying to score points by propelling a rubber ball through a stone hoop without using their hands. The games often had religious undertones and were seen as cosmic battles between light and darkness.

Spectacle and Entertainment

Sporting events in early civilizations were grand spectacles that drew large crowds and served as a form of entertainment. The architecture and infrastructure built to accommodate these events, from Greek stadiums to Roman amphitheaters, were engineering marvels that showcased the importance of sports in society.

The Colosseum

The Roman Colosseum, one of the most iconic structures of antiquity, hosted a wide range of events, from gladiatorial contests to mock sea battles. The amphitheater's capacity to hold up to 80,000 spectators highlights the scale and significance of sporting events in Roman culture.

Greek Stadiums

Greek stadiums, such as the Panathenaic Stadium in Athens, were architectural masterpieces designed for hosting foot races and other athletic competitions. These stadiums were also venues for cultural and religious gatherings.

Social and Cultural Impact

Sporting events in early civilizations had a profound impact on society. They provided a platform for individuals to achieve fame and recognition, and they promoted physical fitness and athleticism among the citizenry.

Civic Pride and Identity

Participation in or victory at sporting events often brought honor and prestige to the competitors and their cities. It fostered a sense of civic pride and identity, and athletes were celebrated as heroes and role models.

Physical and Mental Development

Sporting events promoted physical fitness and mental discipline. Training for competitions encouraged individuals to push their physical and mental limits, resulting in the development of strong and resilient citizens.

Lessons from Early Civilizations

The sporting events of early civilizations remind us that sports have always been a reflection of society, culture, and human aspiration. These events celebrated not only physical prowess but also the values and ideals of the time, from the Greek pursuit of excellence to the Roman appetite for spectacle and entertainment.

In the chapters that follow, we will continue our exploration of the sporting traditions of ancient civilizations and their influence on the development of modern sports.

We will uncover the stories of legendary athletes, examine the rituals and ceremonies surrounding sports, and delve into the profound impact of sports on society. Through this exploration, we will gain a deeper understanding of how the early civilizations of the ancient world laid the foundation for the global sports culture we know today.

So, join us as we journey further into the world of sporting events in early civilizations, where the pursuit of excellence and the thrill of competition have been a timeless source of inspiration and celebration.

Chapter 3: Athleticism in Ancient Egypt

Sporting Activities in Ancient Egyptian Society

Ancient Egypt, with its rich history and cultural heritage, was home to a vibrant tradition of sports and physical activities. Sports were not just pastimes; they played a significant role in Egyptian society, from religious rituals to everyday recreation. In this section, we delve into the diverse world of sporting activities in ancient Egypt and their profound cultural and societal significance.

A Civilization of Athleticism

Athleticism was highly regarded in ancient Egypt, and the civilization celebrated physical fitness and prowess. Sports and physical activities were woven into the fabric of society, shaping both the daily lives of Egyptians and their belief systems.

Physical Fitness and Well-Being

Ancient Egyptians recognized the importance of physical fitness and well-being. Engaging in sports and physical activities was seen as a means of maintaining good health and strength. It was believed that a healthy body was essential for a fruitful life.

Symbolism in Hieroglyphs

Hieroglyphs and inscriptions on ancient Egyptian tombs and monuments often depicted sporting scenes. These depictions served as symbols of vitality, renewal, and the eternal cycle of life, death, and rebirth. Athleticism was not just about the physical; it had deep spiritual and cultural significance.

Sporting Events in Ancient Egypt

The ancient Egyptians engaged in a wide array of sporting events, some of which were highly ritualized and others more recreational. These events provided entertainment, showcased physical prowess, and held religious importance.

Wrestling and Boxing

Wrestling and boxing were popular combat sports in ancient Egypt. Competitions in these sports required strength, agility, and strategy. These events were often part of festivals and celebrations.

Archery and Target Sports

Archery and target sports were important for hunting and warfare. Egyptian archers were renowned for their accuracy, and archery competitions were held to showcase their skill.

Rowing and Water Sports

The Nile River played a central role in Egyptian life, and water sports were common. Rowing contests and swimming races were popular pastimes, often held as part of religious festivals.

Ritual Significance

Many sporting activities in ancient Egypt held deep religious significance. These activities were not just for amusement; they were rituals that honored the gods, expressed gratitude for bountiful harvests, and ensured cosmic order.

The Heb-Sed Festival

The Heb-Sed festival, also known as the Sed festival, was one of the most significant religious events in ancient Egypt. It celebrated the continued rule and vitality of the pharaoh. Sporting events, including foot races, tug-of-war, and archery, were an integral part of this festival.

Horses and Chariots

Horse racing and chariot racing were not only sporting events but also elements of religious ceremonies. These races symbolized the sun god Ra's journey across the sky, and winning a chariot race was seen as a divine blessing.

Everyday Recreation

While some sporting activities in ancient Egypt were reserved for religious or special occasions, others were part of everyday recreation. These activities promoted physical fitness and provided opportunities for social interaction.

Board Games

Board games like Senet and Mehen were popular pastimes. These games required strategy and skill and were often played in social settings.

Ball Games

Ball games were enjoyed by both adults and children. The ancient Egyptians played various ball games, some of which resembled modern sports like soccer and handball.

The Legacy of Ancient Egyptian Sports

The legacy of sports in ancient Egypt can be seen in the enduring appeal of physical activity, physical fitness, and recreation in contemporary society. While the specific sports and rituals have evolved, the fundamental value of staying active and embracing physical prowess continues to be celebrated.

Modern Egyptian Sports

Modern Egypt has its own rich tradition of sports and athletics. Egyptians excel in various sports, including soccer, wrestling, and weightlifting. The passion for sports in Egypt today is a testament to the enduring cultural significance of athleticism.

Lessons from Ancient Egypt

The sporting activities of ancient Egypt remind us that the pursuit of physical fitness and prowess is a timeless human endeavor. These activities were not just about competition but also about celebrating life, honoring the divine, and fostering social bonds. They served as a means of connecting the physical and spiritual aspects of existence.

In the chapters that follow, we will continue our exploration of the role of sports in various ancient civilizations and their influence on the development of modern sports. We will uncover the stories of legendary athletes, examine the rituals and ceremonies surrounding sports, and delve into the profound impact of sports on society. Through this exploration, we will gain a deeper understanding of how the athletic traditions of ancient Egypt have left an indelible mark on the sporting culture of our modern world.

So, join us as we journey further into the world of sporting activities in ancient Egyptian society, where the pursuit of physical excellence and the celebration of life were intertwined with culture and spirituality.

Sporting events as religious ceremonies

In the heart of ancient Egypt, sporting events were not confined to mere competitions; they were elevated to the status of religious ceremonies. These athletic contests were seen as powerful rituals that allowed the ancient Egyptians to connect with the divine, maintain cosmic order, and express their gratitude for the blessings of life. In this section, we delve into the profound religious significance of sporting events in ancient Egypt.

The Spiritual Underpinning

Religion played an integral role in every facet of ancient Egyptian life, and sports were no exception. The ancient Egyptians believed that the physical world and the spiritual realm were deeply interconnected, and sporting events provided a means to bridge the gap between the two.

The Divine Connection

Sports were a way for the ancient Egyptians to honor and connect with their pantheon of gods and goddesses. Many sporting events were dedicated to specific deities, and participants believed that their athletic feats were offerings to the gods.

Ensuring Cosmic Order

The ancient Egyptians held a deep belief in ma'at, the concept of cosmic order and balance. It was believed that the gods maintained ma'at, and human actions had the power to either uphold or disrupt this order. Sporting events, with their structured rules and rituals, were a way to reaffirm ma'at and ensure harmony in the world.

The Heb-Sed Festival

One of the most prominent examples of sporting events with religious significance in ancient Egypt was the Heb-Sed festival, also known as the Sed festival. This grand celebration marked the rejuvenation of the pharaoh's rule and was held after a ruler had been on the throne for thirty years.

Renewal of Pharaonic Power

The Heb-Sed festival was a symbol of the pharaoh's ability to maintain his vitality and effectiveness as a ruler. It was a crucial event that affirmed his divine right to rule and ensured the continued prosperity of Egypt.

Sporting Competitions

Sporting competitions were a central part of the Heb-Sed festival. The pharaoh would participate in various athletic activities, including foot races, tug-of-war, and archery. These contests were not just for entertainment but were rituals that demonstrated the pharaoh's physical prowess and vitality.

Chariot Racing and the Sun God Ra

Chariot racing was another sport with profound religious significance in ancient Egypt. It was believed to symbolize the journey of the sun god Ra across the sky, and winning a chariot race was seen as a divine blessing.

Solar Symbolism

The chariot, drawn by horses, was associated with the sun god Ra, who rode a solar barque across the heavens. Chariot races were held during festivals dedicated to Ra, emphasizing the connection between the sport and the sun god's daily journey.

Divine Favor

Victory in a chariot race was considered a sign of divine favor. Charioteers and their teams were often seen as recipients of Ra's blessings, and their success was attributed to the god's protection.

Sporting Offerings to the Gods

Sports in ancient Egypt were not just about winning; they were offerings to the gods. Competitors believed that their athletic achievements were a form of devotion and a means to seek divine blessings.

Symbolic Rituals

Before and after sporting events, rituals were performed to honor the gods. Participants would offer prayers, libations, and symbolic gestures to invoke divine favor and ensure a successful outcome.

Temples and Offerings

Temples dedicated to specific gods often featured inscriptions and artwork depicting sporting events. These temples served as places of worship where offerings were made to appease the gods associated with the sport.

Lessons from Ancient Egyptian Rituals

The sporting events as religious ceremonies in ancient Egypt serve as a profound reminder of the connection between the physical and the spiritual. They show how sports could be a means of expressing gratitude, ensuring cosmic order, and seeking divine blessings.

In the chapters that follow, we will continue our exploration of the role of sports in various ancient civilizations and their influence on the development of modern sports. We will uncover the stories of legendary athletes, examine the rituals and ceremonies surrounding sports, and delve into the profound impact of sports on society. Through this exploration, we will gain a deeper understanding of how the rituals of ancient Egyptian sports continue to resonate in the world of sports today.

So, join us as we journey further into the world of sporting events as religious ceremonies in ancient Egypt, where athletic prowess and divine connection were intertwined in the pursuit of cosmic harmony and blessings.

Hieroglyphics depicting ancient games

The ancient Egyptians, known for their mastery of hieroglyphic writing, left behind a rich repository of inscriptions and artwork that provide valuable insights into their daily lives, culture, and religious beliefs. Among the myriad subjects immortalized in hieroglyphics, depictions of sports and athletic activities stand as fascinating records of the sporting traditions of ancient Egypt.

Hieroglyphs: The Written Language of Egypt

Hieroglyphs were the written language of ancient Egypt, characterized by intricate symbols that represented words, sounds, and concepts. This sophisticated script was used to record a wide range of information, from religious texts and historical records to poetry and everyday communications.

The Evolution of Hieroglyphs

Hieroglyphic writing evolved over millennia, with the earliest examples dating back to around 3200 BCE. Initially, hieroglyphs were primarily pictorial, but they gradually became more abstract and flexible, allowing for a more extensive range of expression.

Sporting Scenes in Hieroglyphics

Sporting scenes depicted in hieroglyphics offer a unique window into the athletic life of ancient Egypt. These inscriptions capture not only the physical aspects of sports but also the cultural and religious significance they held.

Temple Walls and Tomb Art

Hieroglyphic depictions of sports can be found on the walls of temples, tombs, and monuments. These artworks were not just decorative; they served a multifaceted purpose, including honoring the deceased, celebrating achievements, and preserving cultural traditions.

Symbolism and Ritual

Hieroglyphic representations of sports often carried symbolic and ritualistic connotations. The choice of sports depicted and their accompanying hieroglyphs conveyed deeper meanings related to religion, society, and the afterlife.

The Diversity of Sporting Activities

Hieroglyphics reveal that the ancient Egyptians engaged in a wide variety of sporting activities, each with its unique characteristics and significance.

Wrestling and Boxing

Wrestling and boxing were popular combat sports in ancient Egypt. Hieroglyphic depictions of these sports showcase the techniques, attire, and rituals associated with them. These images provide valuable insights into the physicality and cultural importance of combat sports.

Archery and Hunting

Hieroglyphic inscriptions often feature archers and hunters in action. Archery was not only a sport but also a vital skill for hunting and warfare. These depictions offer glimpses into the equipment, techniques, and strategies employed by archers in ancient Egypt.

Rowing and Water Sports

The Nile River played a central role in Egyptian life, and hieroglyphics depict scenes of rowing contests and other water-related activities. These inscriptions showcase the importance of water sports in daily life and religious ceremonies.

Sporting Ceremonies and Rituals

Hieroglyphic depictions of sporting events often highlight their role in religious ceremonies and festivals.

The Heb-Sed Festival

The Heb-Sed festival, marked by hieroglyphic inscriptions, featured a variety of sporting activities, including foot races and tug-of-war. These inscriptions not only document the physical aspects of the festival but also convey its significance as a renewal of pharaonic power.

Chariot Racing and Solar Symbolism

Hieroglyphic inscriptions related to chariot racing often emphasize its connection to the sun god Ra. These depictions reinforce the belief that chariot races were not mere competitions but symbolic rituals reflecting the journey of the sun across the sky.

Lessons from Hieroglyphic Depictions

The hieroglyphic depictions of ancient Egyptian sports serve as a testament to the enduring cultural significance of athleticism. They remind us that sports were not isolated activities but integral components of daily life, culture, and spirituality.

In the chapters that follow, we will continue our exploration of the role of sports in various ancient civilizations and their influence on the development of modern sports. We will uncover the stories of legendary athletes, examine the rituals and ceremonies surrounding sports, and delve into the profound impact of sports on society. Through this exploration, we will gain a deeper understanding of how the hieroglyphic records of ancient Egyptian sports continue to resonate in the world of sports today.

So, join us as we journey further into the world of hieroglyphics depicting ancient games, where the intricate symbols of an ancient civilization provide a vivid and enduring testament to the role of sports in their culture and history.

Chapter 4: Ancient Greek Panhellenic Games
The significance of the Olympic Games

The Olympic Games, which originated in ancient Greece, stand as one of the most iconic and enduring symbols of athletic competition and human achievement. These games, held in Olympia every four years, were far more than just sporting events. They were a cornerstone of Greek culture, an expression of civic pride, and a celebration of physical excellence. In this section, we delve into the deep significance of the Olympic Games in the ancient Greek world.

A Celebration of Greek Identity

The Olympic Games were a testament to the Greek spirit and identity. They fostered a sense of unity among the Greek city-states, which were often divided by political rivalries and conflicts. During the games, a sacred truce called the "Ekecheiria" was declared, ensuring a period of peace that allowed athletes and spectators to travel to Olympia safely. This temporary cessation of hostilities demonstrated the Greeks' commitment to their shared cultural heritage.

Panhellenic Unity

The Olympics brought together athletes and spectators from all corners of the Greek world, transcending political boundaries. It was a rare opportunity for Greeks to set aside their differences and celebrate their shared history, language, and values.

Honoring the Gods

The Olympic Games were deeply rooted in religious beliefs. The ancient Greeks believed that physical prowess was a gift from the gods, and the Olympics were dedicated to the king of the gods, Zeus. The games were held in Olympia, home to the Temple of Zeus, where a colossal statue of the deity, one of the Seven Wonders of the Ancient World, stood.

Religious Ceremonies

The Olympics began with a grand procession and sacrifices to the gods. Athletes and spectators paid homage to Zeus and sought divine favor for the games. Victors were crowned with olive wreaths, symbolic of the sacred olive tree said to have been planted by Hercules in Olympia.

Zeus' Favor

Winning an Olympic event was seen as a sign of divine favor. Victors were celebrated as heroes, and their achievements were believed to bring honor not only to themselves but also to their city-states and the gods they honored.

Physical and Moral Development

The Olympic Games were a means of promoting physical fitness, mental discipline, and moral character among the Greek citizenry. The pursuit of excellence in sports was seen as a path to becoming a well-rounded and virtuous individual.

Training and Preparation

Competing in the Olympics required rigorous training and discipline. Athletes prepared physically and mentally for years, honing their skills and endurance. This commitment to self-improvement extended beyond sports and into daily life.

Ethical Values

The Greeks believed that participating in sports cultivated virtues such as integrity, perseverance, and sportsmanship. Competitors were expected to adhere to strict codes of fairness and honesty. The Olympics were not just about winning; they were about demonstrating moral character.

Athletic Excellence

The Olympics showcased the pinnacle of athletic achievement in the ancient world. The events encompassed a wide range of disciplines, from foot races to combat sports, and tested the physical prowess of competitors in various ways.

The Primacy of Physicality

Physical prowess was celebrated in ancient Greece, and the Olympics were a stage for athletes to display their strength, speed, and agility. Victors in these competitions were admired as exemplars of human potential.

The Athlete's Journey

The path to becoming an Olympic athlete was arduous, requiring dedication and sacrifice. Training was often conducted in a gymnasium, where athletes practiced under the guidance of trainers and mentors. The physical and mental challenges of training prepared them for the ultimate test in Olympia.

A Lasting Legacy

The Olympic Games left an indelible mark on the world of sports and culture. While the ancient Olympics ceased to exist in their original form, their legacy endures through the modern Olympic Games, which were revived in 1896. The values of unity, excellence, and fair play continue to be celebrated on the global stage.

The Modern Olympics

The revival of the Olympic Games in the modern era was inspired by the principles of the ancient Olympics. The modern Olympics embrace the ideals of international cooperation, athletic excellence, and cultural exchange, embodying the same spirit of unity that characterized the ancient Greek games.

Cultural and Artistic Impact

The Olympic Games have inspired a wide range of artistic and cultural expressions, from literature and art to music and film. The Olympic flame, torch relay, and opening ceremonies are examples of how the symbolism and rituals of the ancient games continue to influence contemporary culture.

Lessons from the Olympic Ideal

The significance of the Olympic Games goes beyond mere athletic competition. They represent the enduring human desire to reach for greatness, to unite in celebration of shared values, and to honor the divine within us. The Olympics remind us that sports have the power to inspire and uplift, transcending boundaries and bringing people together in the pursuit of excellence.

In the chapters that follow, we will continue our exploration of the role of sports in various ancient civilizations and their influence on the development of modern sports. We will uncover the stories of legendary athletes, examine the rituals and ceremonies surrounding sports, and delve into the profound impact of sports on society. Through this exploration, we will gain a deeper understanding of how the significance of the Olympic Games continues to resonate in the world of sports today.

So, join us as we journey further into the world of the Olympic Games, where the pursuit of excellence, unity, and moral character were celebrated on the grandest stage of the ancient Greek world and continue to inspire us today.

Athleticism as an embodiment of Greek values

In ancient Greece, athleticism was not merely a physical pursuit; it was a manifestation of deeply cherished cultural values. The Greek world celebrated physical excellence as a means of cultivating moral character, fostering unity among city-states, and paying homage to the gods. In this section, we delve into how athleticism was an embodiment of Greek values and principles.

Physical Excellence and the Pursuit of Arete

The Greeks held a profound reverence for "arete," a concept that encompassed excellence, virtue, and moral character. Athletics were seen as a means to cultivate and demonstrate arete, both on and off the sporting field.

The Greek Ideal

The Greek ideal of physical excellence, known as "kalokagathia," emphasized the harmony between physical prowess and moral virtue. An individual who possessed physical strength, skill, and beauty was considered to possess inner goodness and excellence as well.

Training for Perfection

Training in the gymnasium was not solely about developing physical strength; it was also about nurturing the mind and spirit. Athletes engaged in a holistic approach to self-improvement, striving for balance in body, mind, and soul.

Moral Character and Sportsmanship

Athletics in ancient Greece were grounded in a strict code of ethics. Competitors were expected to display moral character and sportsmanship, and these values were celebrated as integral to the Olympic ideal.

The Importance of Fair Play

Competing with integrity was paramount in ancient Greek sports. Cheating or unsportsmanlike conduct was met with severe consequences, and athletes who violated these principles were publicly disgraced.

The Agonistic Spirit

The concept of "agon" represented the competitive spirit of Greek athletics. While competition could be fierce, it was also seen as an opportunity to demonstrate virtues such as courage, perseverance, and honor.

Cultural Unity and the Panhellenic Games

The Olympic Games and other Panhellenic Games served as a unifying force among the Greek city-states. These events transcended political rivalries, fostering a sense of cultural unity and shared heritage.

The Olympic Truce

The Ekecheiria, or Olympic truce, was a symbol of unity and peace. It allowed athletes and spectators to travel safely to Olympia, putting aside political conflicts in the spirit of the games.

The Sanctuary of Olympia

The site of Olympia was considered a sacred and neutral ground, where Greeks from all city-states could gather to celebrate their shared values and heritage. The sanctuary became a symbol of cultural unity.

Honoring the Gods and Divine Blessings

The Greeks believed that their physical abilities were gifts from the gods, and athletics provided a means to honor the divine and seek blessings for the community.

The Connection to Zeus

The Olympic Games were dedicated to Zeus, the king of the gods. Victors in these games were seen as recipients of divine favor, and their achievements were considered blessings bestowed by Zeus himself.

Religious Rituals

The Olympics began with religious ceremonies, including sacrifices and prayers to the gods. These rituals were not mere formalities but expressions of gratitude and reverence for divine influence.

Athletic Excellence and Civic Pride

The success of an athlete in ancient Greece brought honor not only to themselves but also to their city-state. Civic pride was closely tied to sporting achievements, and athletes were celebrated as local heroes.

Heroes of the Polis

Athletes were seen as representatives of their city-states, embodying the values and virtues of their communities. Victors returned home as heroes, their names forever etched in the annals of history.

Communal Support

City-states provided financial support, training facilities, and resources to nurture the talents of their athletes. The success of an athlete was a source of pride and validation for the entire community.

The Enduring Legacy

The values celebrated in ancient Greek athletics continue to resonate in the world of sports today. The Olympic ideal of physical excellence, moral character, and cultural unity has left an indelible mark on the global sporting community.

Modern Olympic Movement

The revival of the Olympic Games in the modern era, inspired by the principles of ancient Greece, has expanded the Olympic ideal to a global stage. Today, athletes from all corners of the world come together to celebrate these enduring values.

The Power of Sport

Athletics remain a powerful means of promoting physical fitness, moral character, and cultural unity. Sports have the ability to transcend boundaries and inspire individuals and communities to strive for excellence and unity.

Lessons from Ancient Greek Athleticism

The ancient Greeks recognized the transformative power of athletics, viewing them as a means to cultivate moral character, foster unity, and pay homage to the divine. The Olympic ideal of physical excellence intertwined with moral virtue serves as a timeless reminder of the potential for sports to uplift and inspire.

In the chapters that follow, we will continue our exploration of the role of sports in various ancient civilizations and their influence on the development of modern sports. We will uncover the stories of legendary athletes, examine the rituals and ceremonies surrounding sports, and delve into the profound impact of sports on society. Through this exploration, we will gain a deeper understanding of how the values celebrated through ancient

Greek athleticism continue to shape our contemporary sporting world.

So, join us as we journey further into the world of athletic excellence as an embodiment of Greek values, where physical prowess and moral character were celebrated as twin pillars of human achievement and unity.

Origins of various Greek sports and their rules

The ancient Greeks were passionate about sports and physical competition, and their Panhellenic Games featured a wide array of athletic disciplines. Each sport had its own unique history, cultural significance, and set of rules. In this section, we delve into the origins of various Greek sports and the rules that governed them.

Running and Foot Races

Origins: Foot racing held a prominent place in Greek athletics. The origins of running races can be traced back to the ancient practice of racing for practical purposes, such as messenger running and military training. Over time, these activities evolved into competitive sport.

Rules: The primary foot races in ancient Greece were the stadion (a sprint of approximately 192 meters), the diaulos (a double-stadion race), and the dolichos (races of various longer distances). The rules were simple: athletes had to run in a straight line within their assigned lane, and the first to cross the finish line was declared the winner.

Wrestling

Origins: Wrestling was deeply rooted in Greek culture and had ancient origins in combat training. It was seen as a test of strength, skill, and technique. Wrestling bouts often held spiritual significance and were dedicated to gods like Heracles.

Rules: Greek wrestling had strict rules. Competitors were not allowed to strike or punch their opponents, and holds were limited to those considered safe. Victory was achieved by throwing the opponent to the ground three times, making them touch the ground with their hip, shoulder, or back.

Boxing

Origins: Boxing in ancient Greece had its roots in combat training and was seen as an important skill for warriors. The sport was characterized by its brutality and courage, with fighters using leather thongs wrapped around their fists as rudimentary gloves.

Rules: Boxing matches followed rules to ensure a degree of fairness. Fighters wore a himantes (a type of hand-wrap) and were prohibited from biting, gouging, or hitting below the belt. Matches continued until one fighter either surrendered or was knocked out.

Pankration

Origins: Pankration was a brutal and all-encompassing combat sport that combined elements of wrestling and boxing. It was believed to have originated as a means of military training.

Rules: While pankration was known for its intensity, it had rules. Eye-gouging and biting were forbidden, but almost everything else was allowed, including strikes, holds, and submissions. The objective was to incapacitate the opponent to the point where they surrendered or were unable to continue.

Discus Throwing

Origins: Discus throwing had practical origins in hunting and warfare. The sport involved throwing a heavy discus made of stone or metal for distance.

Rules: The rules for discus throwing were relatively simple. Athletes had to remain within a designated throwing area and were allowed a certain number of steps before releasing the discus. The athlete who threw the discus the farthest was declared the winner.

Javelin Throwing

Origins: Javelin throwing also had its roots in hunting and warfare, with the javelin being used as a weapon. The sport required both strength and precision.

Rules: The rules of javelin throwing were straightforward. Athletes had to throw the javelin from within a designated area and were not allowed to cross a specified line. The athlete who threw the javelin the farthest won.

Long Jump

Origins: The long jump was inspired by practical activities like leaping across streams and ditches. It evolved into a sport that tested an athlete's jumping ability.

Rules: Athletes had to jump from a standing position and land in a designated sand pit. The distance from the takeoff point to the landing point determined the winner. Fouls were called if an athlete overstepped the takeoff line or failed to land in the pit.

Chariot Racing

Origins: Chariot racing was one of the most prestigious and dramatic events in Greek athletics. It likely had origins in military training and eventually became an integral part of religious festivals.

Rules: Chariot racing involved chariots drawn by teams of horses. The objective was to complete a set number of laps around a circular track. The charioteer who crossed the finish line first was declared the victor. The sport was known for its danger and required exceptional skill.

The Pentathlon

Origins: The pentathlon was a combination of five events: discus throwing, long jump, javelin throwing, stadion (a foot race), and wrestling. It was believed to have originated as a test of an athlete's overall abilities.

Rules: The pentathlon had a complex scoring system. Points were awarded based on performance in each event, with the athlete who accumulated the most points declared the winner. This event required a well-rounded skill set.

The Decathlon

Origins: The decathlon, while not part of the ancient Greek games, is worth mentioning due to its modern counterpart. It consists of ten events, including sprints, distance running, throwing, jumping, and hurdling. The decathlon has its origins in ancient pentathlon contests.

Rules: In the modern decathlon, athletes accumulate points across ten events, with the winner being the athlete with the highest total score. Each event has specific rules and scoring criteria.

Legacy and Influence

The sports of ancient Greece continue to influence modern athletics and the Olympic Games. Many of the principles, values, and rules that guided these ancient competitions remain relevant today, emphasizing the enduring legacy of Greek sports.

In the chapters that follow, we will continue our exploration of the role of sports in various ancient civilizations and their influence on the development of modern sports. We will uncover the stories of legendary athletes, examine the rituals and ceremonies surrounding sports, and delve into the profound impact of sports on society. Through this exploration, we will gain a deeper understanding of how the origins and rules of various Greek sports continue to shape the world of sports today.

So, join us as we journey further into the world of ancient Greek sports, where the pursuit of physical excellence and adherence to rules were celebrated as expressions of cultural values and human potential.

Chapter 5: The Roman Arena and Beyond
Gladiatorial contests and chariot races

The Roman arena stands as an iconic symbol of ancient spectacle and entertainment. Within its sand-covered floors, the Romans celebrated a wide array of events, with gladiatorial contests and chariot races taking center stage. In this section, we explore the origins, cultural significance, and rules of these two gripping forms of entertainment.

Gladiatorial Contests

Origins: The origins of gladiatorial combat can be traced back to ancient Etruria, where funeral games featured fights to honor the deceased. The Romans adopted and adapted this practice, transforming it into a form of mass entertainment.

Cultural Significance: Gladiatorial contests became deeply ingrained in Roman culture. These brutal spectacles served various purposes, including honoring gods, celebrating military victories, and entertaining the populace. They also reflected Roman values of discipline, courage, and the importance of physical prowess.

Types of Gladiators: The Roman arena featured a diverse array of gladiator types, each with their unique weapons and fighting styles. Examples include the retiarius (net-fighter), secutor (chaser), and murmillo (fisherman). Each type had its own set of fans and tactics.

Rules: While gladiatorial combat was undoubtedly brutal, it was not without rules. Referees oversaw the matches, and fighters were bound by certain regulations. The death of a gladiator was typically the result of a thumb gesture from the referee or the will of the crowd.

Training and Life of Gladiators: Gladiators underwent rigorous training, often in specialized schools (ludi). They were treated as property and typically fought for fame, fortune, or freedom. Some gladiators became celebrated heroes, while others faced a life of hardship and exploitation.

Chariot Races

Origins: Chariot racing had ancient origins in Greece, but it reached its zenith in the Roman Empire. The sport evolved from practical uses, such as transportation and warfare, into a thrilling spectacle.

Cultural Significance: Chariot racing was one of the most popular and enduring forms of entertainment in ancient Rome. The Circus Maximus in Rome could accommodate over a quarter of a million spectators, highlighting its cultural significance. Chariot races were often associated with specific gods, and their outcomes were believed to have divine implications.

Types of Races: Chariot races came in various forms, with quadrigae (four-horse chariots) and bigae (two-horse chariots) being the most common. Races took place in a circus, an oval-shaped arena with a central spina (barrier) around which the chariots raced.

Rules: Chariot races had their own set of rules and regulations. Fouls and collisions were common, but there were limits on dangerous maneuvers. The race was won by the charioteer who completed the designated number of laps first, often involving seven laps for quadrigae races.

Factions and Rivalries: Chariot racing was organized into factions, represented by different colors (Red, Blue, Green, and White). These factions had loyal fan bases and often stirred fierce rivalries. Charioteers became celebrities, and chariot racing was not just a sport but a way of life for many.

Dangers and Rewards: Chariot racing was a perilous occupation, with frequent accidents and injuries. However, successful charioteers could amass great wealth and fame. The sport was known for its unpredictability, and fortunes could change in an instant.

The Legacy of Roman Spectacle

The gladiatorial contests and chariot races of ancient Rome left an indelible mark on the world of entertainment and sport. While they were products of their time, these spectacles continue to captivate modern audiences and inspire works of art, literature, and film.

Cultural Reflection: Gladiatorial contests and chariot races mirrored the values, aspirations, and idiosyncrasies of Roman society. They embodied themes of valor, rivalry, sacrifice, and the allure of fame.

Entertainment Evolution: The Roman fascination with spectacle influenced the development of modern sports and entertainment. Elements of gladiatorial combat and chariot racing can be seen in contemporary combat sports and motorsport.

Modern Revivals: The spirit of Roman spectacle endures in various forms. Today, historical reenactments, movies, and TV series pay homage to the gladiators and charioteers who once captivated the masses.

In the chapters that follow, we will continue our exploration of the role of sports in various ancient civilizations and their influence on the development of modern sports. We will uncover the stories of legendary athletes, examine the rituals and ceremonies surrounding sports, and delve into the profound impact of sports on society. Through this exploration, we will gain a deeper understanding of how the spectacles of ancient Rome continue to shape the world of sports and entertainment today.

So, join us as we journey further into the world of gladiatorial contests and chariot races, where the roar of the crowd and the thrill of competition reverberate through the annals of history and inspire us to this day.

Roman influence on sports culture

Ancient Rome, with its vast empire and rich cultural heritage, left an enduring mark on the world of sports. The Romans embraced various athletic endeavors and integrated them into their daily lives, influencing not only their own society but also the development of sports culture in subsequent civilizations. In this section, we delve into the profound Roman influence on sports culture.

The Roman Love for Spectacle

Roman culture celebrated grandeur, and sports were no exception. The Romans had a passion for public spectacles and entertainment that extended from the circus to the arena. These extravagant events became deeply ingrained in Roman society, setting the stage for a legacy of sports spectacle.

The Circus Maximus

The Circus Maximus was one of the most iconic arenas in ancient Rome, dedicated primarily to chariot racing. It could accommodate an astounding number of spectators, reflecting the Romans' enthusiasm for large-scale sporting events.

The Colosseum

The Colosseum, also known as the Flavian Amphitheatre, stands as a symbol of Roman engineering and entertainment. This colossal arena hosted gladiatorial contests, animal hunts, and mock sea battles, captivating audiences with its grandeur and brutality.

Public Games

Roman emperors and officials sponsored public games (ludi publici) as a means of maintaining social order and ensuring the loyalty of the populace. These games encompassed a wide range of sports, from athletics and chariot racing to gladiatorial combat.

Roman Athletics and Sportsmanship

The Romans inherited much of their athletic tradition from the Greeks but added their own distinctive flavor. Athletics in Rome promoted physical fitness, discipline, and sportsmanship, embodying Roman values and ideals.

The Gymnasium

Roman gymnasia, like their Greek counterparts, served as training grounds for athletes. These facilities offered not only physical training but also education in literature, philosophy, and culture.

Competitions and Festivals

Roman cities held local athletic competitions and festivals (agones) that mirrored Greek traditions. These events included foot races, wrestling, boxing, and various field sports, promoting camaraderie and sportsmanship among participants.

The Roman Ideal

The Roman ideal of "a sound mind in a sound body" emphasized the harmonious development of both mental and physical faculties. It encouraged citizens to engage in regular physical exercise to maintain health and vigor.

The Influence of Roman Games on Later Sports

Roman sports and games have left a lasting imprint on the development of modern sports and entertainment. Many aspects of Roman sports culture continue to influence contemporary athletic events.

Gladiatorial Combat

The spectacle of gladiatorial combat, while gruesome, captivated audiences. Elements of gladiatorial combat can be seen in contemporary combat sports like boxing, MMA (Mixed Martial Arts), and professional wrestling.

Chariot Racing

Chariot racing, with its dramatic races and passionate fan base, laid the groundwork for modern motorsports like Formula 1 and NASCAR. The concept of racing in circuses is a direct legacy of Roman chariot races.

Sporting Arenas

The design and architecture of Roman sports arenas have influenced the construction of modern stadiums and arenas, from the Colosseum's iconic elliptical shape to the layout of seating and spectator facilities.

The Olympic Ideal

The modern Olympic Games draw inspiration from the values celebrated in ancient Greek and Roman athletics. Concepts like fair competition, sportsmanship, and unity among nations echo the ideals of the ancient world.

The Enduring Legacy

The Roman influence on sports culture is not confined to a bygone era but continues to shape contemporary sporting events, traditions, and values. The legacy of Rome's sporting heritage is a testament to the enduring power of sports to unite, entertain, and inspire.

Sporting Rituals and Ceremonies

The opening ceremonies, torch relays, and medal presentations of modern Olympic Games are steeped in symbolism reminiscent of ancient rituals, connecting past and present.

Global Sporting Events

The organization and staging of international sporting events, from the FIFA World Cup to the Summer and Winter

Olympics, reflect the grandeur and spectacle celebrated in Roman games.

The Values of Sportsmanship

The emphasis on sportsmanship, fair play, and the pursuit of excellence, which were integral to Roman athletics, continue to be cherished principles in the world of sports today.

The Love for Spectacle

The Roman fascination with spectacle and the role of the spectator in shaping sporting events have persisted, as evidenced by the passion of modern sports fans and the global reach of sports broadcasts.

Conclusion: A Sporting Heritage

The Roman influence on sports culture remains an enduring legacy that transcends time and borders. From the grand arenas of ancient Rome to the global stage of contemporary sports, the principles, values, and love for spectacle cultivated in Roman society continue to shape and enrich the world of athletics.

In the chapters that follow, we will continue our exploration of the role of sports in various ancient civilizations and their influence on the development of modern sports. We will uncover the stories of legendary athletes, examine the rituals and ceremonies surrounding sports, and delve into the profound impact of sports on society. Through this exploration, we will gain a deeper understanding of how the Roman love for spectacle and the values of sportsmanship continue to resonate in the world of sports today.

So, join us as we journey further into the realm of Roman influence on sports culture, where the legacy of grandeur, discipline, and entertainment continues to inspire athletes and spectators alike.

Spread of Roman-style amphitheaters and games

The grandeur of Roman amphitheaters and the allure of the games held within them were not confined to the city of Rome alone. As the Roman Empire expanded, so too did its cultural influence, including the tradition of building amphitheaters and staging spectacular events. In this section, we explore the spread of Roman-style amphitheaters and games throughout the vast reaches of the empire.

Amphitheaters as Cultural Icons

Roman amphitheaters were architectural marvels, designed not only for their functionality but also for their aesthetic appeal. These elliptical arenas, with their tiered seating and impressive facades, became symbols of Roman culture and civilization.

Iconic Amphitheaters

The Colosseum (Flavian Amphitheatre): Rome's most famous amphitheater, the Colosseum, was a model for subsequent constructions. It stood as a testament to Roman engineering and remains an iconic symbol of the ancient world.

The Arena of Nîmes: Located in what is now France, the Arena of Nîmes is one of the best-preserved Roman amphitheaters. Its elliptical shape and tiered seating showcase Roman architectural innovation.

The Pula Arena: Situated in Croatia, the Pula Arena is another well-preserved Roman amphitheater. It continues to host various events and serves as a living testament to Roman influence in the region.

The Romanization of Entertainment

As the Roman Empire expanded its territories, it brought with it not only its architecture but also its cultural practices. Roman-style amphitheaters and the games they hosted began to appear in regions far beyond the Italian Peninsula.

Provincial Amphitheaters

Provence, France: The province of Gaul, which included modern-day France, was home to several Roman amphitheaters. Nîmes, Arles, and Lyon, among others, boasted arenas where gladiatorial contests and chariot races entertained the local population.

North Africa: Roman amphitheaters sprang up in North African cities such as Carthage (modern-day Tunisia) and Thysdrus (modern-day El Djem, Tunisia). These arenas hosted events that mirrored those in Rome.

The Balkans: Amphitheaters were constructed in various cities across the Balkans, including Pula in Croatia, Sofia in Bulgaria, and Thessaloniki in Greece. These arenas became hubs of entertainment and culture.

Cultural Exchange

The spread of amphitheaters and games went hand in hand with cultural exchange. Romanization influenced local customs and traditions, and provincial populations embraced the spectacle and excitement of Roman-style entertainment.

The Adaptation of Local Traditions

While Roman-style amphitheaters became fixtures in many regions, they often coexisted with local traditions and practices. In some cases, Roman games were adapted to incorporate elements of local culture and religious beliefs.

Religious Festivals

In some provinces, amphitheater events were incorporated into religious festivals and ceremonies. These festivities blended Roman and indigenous practices, creating unique and culturally rich spectacles.

Regional Variations

Local populations sometimes introduced variations to the games. For example, chariot racing in the Byzantine Empire had distinct characteristics and rituals compared to its Roman predecessor.

Syncretism in Entertainment

The syncretism of cultures in the provinces led to diverse and dynamic forms of entertainment. It showcased the resilience and adaptability of Roman-style amphitheaters and games.

The Enduring Legacy

The legacy of Roman-style amphitheaters and games extends far beyond the borders of the ancient Roman Empire. Today, these iconic structures and the entertainment they once hosted continue to captivate and inspire people around the world.

Preservation and Restoration

Many Roman amphitheaters have been preserved or restored and are now tourist attractions, cultural landmarks, and venues for modern events. Their enduring presence connects contemporary society to the ancient world.

Influence on Architecture

The architectural innovations introduced by the Romans in amphitheater design have influenced subsequent generations of builders and architects. Modern stadiums and arenas owe a debt to the ingenuity of Roman engineering.

Cultural Exchange

The spread of Roman-style amphitheaters and games exemplifies the power of cultural exchange. It highlights how traditions can travel and adapt, leaving a lasting impact on the cultural heritage of various regions.

Sports and Spectacle

The Roman love for spectacle and entertainment, evident in their amphitheaters and games, has transcended time and continues to shape contemporary sports culture and entertainment.

In the chapters that follow, we will continue our exploration of the role of sports in various ancient civilizations and their influence on the development of modern sports. We will uncover the stories of legendary athletes, examine the rituals and ceremonies surrounding sports, and delve into the profound impact of sports on society. Through this exploration, we will gain a deeper understanding of how the spread of Roman-style amphitheaters and games contributed to the rich tapestry of global sporting culture.

So, join us as we journey further into the world of Roman influence, where the architectural splendor of amphitheaters and the thrill of the games continue to echo through the annals of history and inspire us to this day.

Chapter 6: Indigenous Sports and Ancient Americas
Sports in Native American societies

The indigenous peoples of the Americas, spanning diverse cultures, landscapes, and histories, had a rich tradition of sports and athletic activities long before the arrival of European settlers. These sports were not only physical contests but also integral parts of tribal life, often carrying spiritual, social, and cultural significance. In this section, we delve into the fascinating world of sports in Native American societies.

The Cultural Significance of Native American Sports

Sports and athletic competitions held profound meaning in Native American societies, serving multiple purposes beyond mere entertainment. They were deeply ingrained in tribal customs, reflecting the values, beliefs, and traditions of each indigenous group.

Spiritual Connections

Many Native American sports had spiritual connections. For example, the Hopi people of the American Southwest engaged in foot racing as a form of prayer and meditation, believing it brought rain and fertility to their crops.

Social Cohesion

Sports played a crucial role in fostering unity and cooperation within tribes. Competitions provided opportunities for individuals to showcase their skills, while also reinforcing tribal bonds and identity.

Cultural Celebration

Tribal gatherings and festivals often featured athletic contests as part of their celebrations. These events allowed tribes to showcase their cultural heritage and share it with neighboring groups.

A Diverse Array of Sports

The indigenous peoples of the Americas had a wide variety of sports and athletic activities that reflected the regions they inhabited, their available resources, and their unique cultural practices. Here are some notable examples:

Lacrosse

Lacrosse, known as the "Creator's Game," was played by many Native American tribes across North America. It was more than just a sport; it was a spiritual activity with ceremonial aspects. The game involved using a long-handled stick with a netted pocket to catch and throw a ball, with the objective of scoring goals.

Chunkey

Chunkey was a game played by the Mississippian culture in what is now the southeastern United States. It involved rolling a stone disc along the ground and then throwing spears to where the disc would stop. It combined skill and precision with physical agility.

Foot Racing

Foot racing was a common sport among many Native American tribes. Different regions had their variations, such as the Tarahumara runners of Mexico and the Hopi foot racers of the American Southwest. These races often had cultural or religious significance.

Stickball

Similar to lacrosse, stickball was a popular sport in Native American communities, especially in the Southeastern United States. It was played with long sticks with nets, and teams competed to score goals. Stickball games were often associated with community gatherings and ceremonies.

Patolli

Patolli was a traditional board game played by various Mesoamerican cultures, including the Aztecs and the Maya. The game involved moving pieces along a cross-shaped board, with a focus on strategy and luck. It served both as entertainment and a form of divination.

Sports and the Changing Landscape

The arrival of European settlers in the Americas brought about significant changes in Native American societies, including their sports and athletic traditions. Contact with Europeans introduced new games, sports equipment, and even horses, which had a transformative effect on tribal life.

Influence of European Sports

Native American tribes, such as the Cherokee and Choctaw, adopted European-style ball games like soccer and rugby. These games integrated into tribal culture while retaining some indigenous elements.

The Introduction of Horses

The introduction of horses by Europeans revolutionized Plains Indian cultures. Horse racing and equestrian sports became popular, offering new opportunities for competition and trade.

Persistence of Tradition

Despite the profound changes brought by colonization, many Native American sports and games endured. Tribes worked to preserve their cultural heritage, and today, efforts continue to revive and celebrate these traditions.

Contemporary Revival and Preservation

In recent decades, there has been a resurgence of interest in Native American sports and games. Tribes and indigenous organizations have made concerted efforts to revive and preserve these cultural treasures.

Indigenous Games

The North American Indigenous Games (NAIG) and the World Indigenous Games have provided platforms for indigenous athletes to showcase their skills and celebrate their cultural heritage on a global stage.

Cultural Centers and Education

Cultural centers, museums, and educational programs have played a crucial role in preserving and sharing the history and significance of Native American sports with younger generations.

Sporting Events and Festivals

Annual events and festivals celebrate Native American sports and culture. These gatherings serve as opportunities for tribes to come together, share their traditions, and introduce others to their sports.

Conclusion: A Rich Sporting Heritage

The sports of Native American societies represent a vital and diverse aspect of indigenous culture. They embody the values of unity, spirituality, and tradition. As these sports continue to be celebrated and shared, they serve as a testament to the resilience and enduring legacy of Native American cultures.

In the chapters that follow, we will continue our exploration of the role of sports in various ancient civilizations and their influence on the development of modern sports. We will uncover the stories of legendary athletes, examine the rituals and ceremonies surrounding sports, and delve into the profound impact of sports on society. Through this exploration, we will gain a deeper understanding of how Native American sports and traditions continue to inspire and enrich the world of sports today.

So, join us as we journey further into the world of Native American sports, where the echoes of ancient games and the spirit of cultural preservation continue to thrive in the modern era.

Ball games of Mesoamerica and South America

The ancient civilizations of Mesoamerica and South America, known for their architectural marvels, complex societies, and rich cultural traditions, also had a deep affinity for sports and games. Among their diverse athletic activities, ball games held a central place, blending physical prowess, ritual significance, and entertainment. In this section, we delve into the captivating world of ball games in these regions.

The Sacred Ball Game

Ball games in Mesoamerica and South America were more than just pastimes; they were often imbued with spiritual and ritualistic elements. The rules and symbolism varied among different cultures, but common themes included a rubber ball, stone courts, and a blend of athleticism and tradition.

The Maya Ballgame

The Maya, known for their sophisticated civilization in present-day Mexico and Central America, had a particularly well-documented ballgame. The game, known as "pok-ta-pok" or "ulama," was played in stone ball courts. Players used their hips, shoulders, and forearms to strike a solid rubber ball, attempting to score points by getting the ball through stone rings or markers.

Ritual Significance: The Maya ballgame had profound religious and ritualistic meaning. It often symbolized the journey of the sun through the underworld, with players representing the gods. The outcome of the game had cosmic implications, impacting agricultural cycles and the prosperity of the Maya people.

Sacrificial Elements: Some versions of the Maya ballgame were deadly. The losing team, and sometimes even the winning team's captain, could face ritual sacrifice. This aspect added an element of gravity to the game, emphasizing its role in Mayan spirituality.

The Aztec Ballgame

The Aztecs, who built a vast empire in Central Mexico, had their own version of the ballgame called "tlachtli." Like the Maya game, tlachtli was played on stone courts with a rubber ball. However, there were variations in rules and symbolism.

Symbol of Warfare: The Aztecs viewed tlachtli as a reflection of the cosmic struggle between light and darkness. The game was also associated with warfare, and sometimes prisoners of war were forced to play, with the grim knowledge that the losers could be sacrificed.

Courts as Sacred Spaces: Aztec ball courts were often considered sacred spaces. The architecture incorporated religious symbols, and the courts were used for ceremonies and offerings to the gods.

The Incan Ball Game

In the Andean region of South America, the Inca civilization developed its own form of ball game. Known as "tlakwa" or "panqatapa," this game was played on rectangular courts with teams of players who aimed to score points by propelling a ball made of animal bladders through a hoop.

Physical and Social Activity: The Incan ball game served both as a physical activity and a means of social interaction. Teams could consist of family members, and the game promoted camaraderie and competition.

Cultural Festivals: Tlakwa was often part of larger cultural festivals and celebrations, showcasing the Incan emphasis on communal activities and the importance of tradition.

Legacy and Revival

While the civilizations of Mesoamerica and South America that played these ball games are ancient, their legacy continues to resonate in the modern world.

Contemporary Play

Efforts to revive and preserve traditional ball games are ongoing in indigenous communities. Tournaments and exhibitions provide opportunities for people to connect with their cultural heritage.

Archaeological Insights

Archaeological excavations of ball courts and related artifacts offer valuable insights into the rules, equipment, and symbolism of these ancient games.

Cultural Significance

The enduring cultural significance of these ball games underscores their importance in the history and identity of indigenous peoples in Mesoamerica and South America.

Conclusion: A Sporting Heritage

The ball games of Mesoamerica and South America represent a unique intersection of sport, spirituality, and tradition. These games, with their deep-rooted cultural significance, continue to captivate and inspire, serving as a testament to the enduring legacy of ancient civilizations.

In the chapters that follow, we will continue our exploration of the role of sports in various ancient civilizations and their influence on the development of modern sports. We will uncover the stories of legendary athletes, examine the rituals and ceremonies surrounding sports, and delve into the profound impact of sports on society. Through this exploration, we will gain a deeper understanding of how the ball games of Mesoamerica and

South America continue to echo through the annals of history and inspire us to this day.

So, join us as we journey further into the world of indigenous sports, where the ancient echoes of athleticism and cultural richness continue to thrive in the modern era.

Cultural and spiritual dimensions of indigenous sports

Sports and athletic activities in indigenous societies of the Americas were not merely physical contests but integral components of their cultural and spiritual heritage. These activities held profound meaning, connecting individuals, communities, and the cosmos. In this section, we delve into the captivating cultural and spiritual dimensions of indigenous sports.

Sports as Cultural Expression

Indigenous sports were a reflection of the diverse cultures, traditions, and values of native peoples throughout the Americas. Each game and athletic activity had its unique cultural significance and served as a means of expression for indigenous communities.

Ritual and Ceremony

Many indigenous sports were intertwined with rituals and ceremonies. They often marked important events, such as harvests, solstices, or transitions in life, and were an essential part of communal celebrations.

Symbolism in Play

The rules, equipment, and movements in indigenous sports often carried symbolic meanings. For example, the circular shape of some ball courts mirrored the cyclical nature of life and the cosmos.

Cultural Identity

Participating in these sports instilled a sense of cultural pride and identity. They reinforced the values and traditions of each indigenous group and fostered a connection to ancestral heritage.

Spiritual Dimensions

Indigenous sports were deeply rooted in spiritual beliefs and cosmologies. They were seen as more than physical activities; they were avenues for spiritual connection and understanding of the world.

Sacred Spaces

Ball courts and playing fields were often considered sacred spaces. They were meticulously designed with cosmological principles in mind and sometimes featured altars or offerings to honor the spirits.

Spiritual Guardians

Some indigenous sports involved invoking the aid of spiritual guardians or deities. Participants sought blessings for success and protection from harm during play.

Cosmic Symbolism

The movements and rules of indigenous sports often mirrored cosmological concepts. For instance, the movement of a ball in a ballgame might symbolize the sun's journey across the sky.

Communal and Social Significance

Indigenous sports were communal events that brought people together. They fostered cooperation, communication, and shared experiences within tribes and between neighboring communities.

Cooperation and Unity

Team-based sports, like indigenous ball games, encouraged teamwork and cooperation. Players had to work together for the collective good of their community.

Social Cohesion

Sports events often included entire communities, reinforcing social bonds and interdependence among tribal members. These gatherings were occasions for feasting, dancing, and storytelling.

Transmission of Knowledge

Indigenous sports served as educational tools, transmitting cultural knowledge, stories, and traditions from one generation to the next. Elders often played a role in passing down the skills and values associated with these activities.

Legacy and Revival

The cultural and spiritual dimensions of indigenous sports continue to resonate in the modern world. Efforts to revive and preserve these traditions are ongoing, ensuring that their significance endures.

Contemporary Play

Indigenous communities organize tournaments and exhibitions to keep traditional sports alive. These events provide opportunities for people to reconnect with their cultural heritage.

Cultural Centers and Education

Cultural centers, museums, and educational programs play a crucial role in preserving and sharing the history and significance of indigenous sports with younger generations.

Cultural Pride

Participation in indigenous sports fosters a sense of cultural pride and identity among indigenous youth, strengthening their connection to their heritage.

Conclusion: A Sacred Legacy

Indigenous sports in the Americas are more than just games; they are sacred legacies that embody the cultural, spiritual, and communal values of native peoples. These sports serve as a testament to the enduring resilience of indigenous cultures and their profound connection to the natural and spiritual worlds.

In the chapters that follow, we will continue our exploration of the role of sports in various ancient civilizations and their influence on the development of modern sports. We will uncover the stories of legendary athletes, examine the rituals and ceremonies surrounding sports, and delve into the profound impact of sports on society. Through this exploration, we will gain a deeper understanding of how the cultural and spiritual dimensions of indigenous sports continue to echo through the annals of history and inspire us to this day.

So, join us as we journey further into the world of indigenous sports, where the echoes of ancient traditions and the spirit of cultural preservation continue to thrive in the modern era.

Chapter 7: Sporting Traditions of the Far East

Ancient Chinese martial arts and competitions

Martial arts have a long and storied history in China, dating back thousands of years. These ancient practices, encompassing a wide range of fighting techniques and philosophies, played a significant role in Chinese culture, society, and sport. In this section, we delve into the fascinating world of ancient Chinese martial arts and competitions.

Origins and Development

Chinese martial arts, often referred to as "kung fu" or "wushu," have their roots in antiquity. The development of these martial traditions can be traced to various sources, including military training, self-defense techniques, and philosophical teachings.

Military Origins

Ancient China's feudal states and frequent conflicts led to the development of military strategies and combat techniques. Soldiers were trained in martial skills to defend their territories and engage in warfare effectively.

Taoist and Buddhist Influences

Taoist and Buddhist monks also played a significant role in the development of martial arts. Monasteries served as centers of knowledge where monks explored physical and mental disciplines, including combat techniques.

Philosophical Foundations

Chinese martial arts were not merely about physical combat; they were deeply intertwined with philosophy. Concepts such as Taoism's "softness overcomes hardness" and Confucian values of discipline and virtue influenced the principles of martial arts.

Styles and Schools

Over centuries, various styles and schools of Chinese martial arts emerged, each with its unique techniques, forms, and philosophies. These styles often bear the names of their founders or originators.

Shaolin Kung Fu

The Shaolin Temple in Henan Province is legendary for its role in the development of martial arts. Shaolin Kung Fu emphasizes physical conditioning, flexibility, and a wide range of combat techniques.

Tai Chi

Tai Chi, also known as Taijiquan, is renowned for its slow and flowing movements. It combines martial techniques with health benefits and is often practiced for its meditative qualities.

Wing Chun

Wing Chun is a close-range martial art known for its efficiency and simplicity. It is famous for its focus on practical self-defense techniques and rapid strikes.

Baguazhang

Baguazhang, or "Eight Trigrams Palm," incorporates circular movements and intricate footwork. It emphasizes fluidity, evasion, and the use of leverage in combat.

Philosophical and Spiritual Aspects

Chinese martial arts are not solely about physical combat; they encompass philosophical and spiritual dimensions that emphasize balance, discipline, and personal growth.

Mind-Body Connection

Practitioners of Chinese martial arts often stress the importance of a strong mind-body connection. Techniques are performed with mindfulness and focus on breathing and energy flow.

Harmony with Nature

Chinese martial arts draw inspiration from the natural world, incorporating animal-like movements and imitating the forces of nature. This connection to the environment reflects Taoist philosophy.

Self-Cultivation

Martial arts in China have long been associated with self-cultivation and personal development. They offer a path to physical fitness, mental clarity, and spiritual growth.

Martial Arts Competitions

Throughout history, martial arts competitions and demonstrations were held in China as a means of testing and showcasing martial skills. These competitions were not only displays of physical prowess but also opportunities for cultural exchange.

Lei Tai Competitions

Lei Tai, or "raised platform," competitions date back to ancient times. Fighters would engage in combat on an elevated platform, showcasing their martial skills and techniques.

Exhibitions and Demonstrations

Martial artists would often perform demonstrations to share their knowledge and skills with the public. These events served as both entertainment and educational opportunities.

Contemporary Competitions

In modern times, traditional martial arts competitions are held both in China and around the world. These events feature forms, sparring, and various disciplines, allowing practitioners to test their skills and compete for recognition.

Legacy and Global Influence

The legacy of ancient Chinese martial arts extends far beyond China's borders. These traditions have influenced martial arts practices worldwide and continue to be celebrated for their rich history and philosophical depth.

Global Reach

Chinese martial arts, including Tai Chi and Kung Fu, have gained popularity worldwide. They are practiced not only for self-defense but also for fitness, stress relief, and personal development.

Integration into Popular Culture

Martial arts movies, such as those featuring Bruce Lee and Jackie Chan, have played a significant role in introducing Chinese martial arts to global audiences and shaping their perception.

Cultural Exchange

Chinese martial arts have served as a medium for cultural exchange, with practitioners from different countries traveling to China to learn and share their knowledge.

Conclusion: A Timeless Tradition

Ancient Chinese martial arts are a testament to the enduring legacy of physical, philosophical, and spiritual disciplines. These practices continue to inspire and enrich the world of martial arts and serve as a bridge between physical prowess and inner harmony.

In the chapters that follow, we will continue our exploration of the role of sports in various ancient civilizations and their influence on the development of modern sports. We will uncover the stories of legendary athletes, examine the rituals and ceremonies surrounding sports, and delve into the profound impact of sports on society. Through this exploration, we will gain a deeper understanding of how ancient Chinese martial arts and their philosophy continue to echo through the annals of history and inspire us to this day.

So, join us as we journey further into the world of ancient Chinese martial arts, where the wisdom of the past continues to guide the way forward.

Martial arts in Japanese culture

Japan's martial arts, collectively known as "budo," hold a unique and revered place within the nation's culture and history. Rooted in ancient traditions, martial arts in Japan encompass a wide range of disciplines, each with its philosophy, techniques, and principles. In this section, we delve into the profound influence of martial arts on Japanese culture.

Historical Development

The evolution of Japanese martial arts is intertwined with the country's rich history and samurai heritage. These martial traditions developed over centuries, shaped by the social, political, and philosophical changes in Japan.

Samurai Origins

The samurai, Japan's warrior class, played a pivotal role in the development of martial arts. They required effective combat skills for their roles as protectors and enforcers.

Feudal Japan

Feudal Japan's turbulent history of warring states fostered the development of various martial disciplines. Schools of combat, known as "ryuha," emerged to teach specific techniques.

Influence of Zen Buddhism

Zen Buddhism had a profound impact on Japanese martial arts. It emphasized discipline, meditation, and the cultivation of a calm mind, which became integral to martial training.

Key Martial Arts Disciplines

Japanese martial arts encompass a wide array of disciplines, each with its unique techniques, philosophies, and purposes. Some of the most prominent martial arts in Japan include:

Judo

Founded by Jigoro Kano in the late 19th century, Judo emphasizes throws and grappling techniques. It is known for its principle of "maximum efficiency, minimum effort."

Karate

Karate, originally from Okinawa, focuses on striking techniques, including punches, kicks, and knee strikes. It places a strong emphasis on discipline and self-control.

Kendo

Kendo, the "way of the sword," is a modern martial art derived from traditional samurai swordsmanship. Practitioners use bamboo swords and protective armor.

Aikido

Aikido, developed by Morihei Ueshiba, is a martial art centered on using an opponent's energy and movements to control or redirect their attacks. It emphasizes harmony and non-violence.

Kyudo

Kyudo, or Japanese archery, is a highly ritualized martial art that emphasizes perfect form and mental focus. It is often described as a path to self-improvement.

Philosophical and Spiritual Aspects

Japanese martial arts are deeply imbued with philosophical and spiritual dimensions. They encompass more than physical combat; they serve as pathways to self-improvement and personal development.

Bushido: The Way of the Warrior

Bushido, the "way of the warrior," is a code of ethics that guided samurai conduct. It emphasizes virtues like loyalty, honor, and integrity.

Zen and Martial Arts

Zen Buddhism's influence on martial arts is profound. Meditation, mindfulness, and the cultivation of a clear mind are integral to many martial practices.

Discipline and Self-Control

Martial arts in Japan emphasize discipline, self-control, and respect for one's training partners and opponents. These principles extend beyond the dojo (training hall) into daily life.

Martial Arts in Modern Japan

Martial arts continue to be an integral part of modern Japanese culture. They have evolved to include competitive sports and have garnered international recognition.

Sports Competitions

Many martial arts, including Judo and Karate, have become popular competitive sports, with international tournaments and Olympic recognition.

Cultural Export

Japanese martial arts have been exported worldwide, contributing to Japan's cultural influence globally. They are practiced for fitness, self-defense, and personal development.

Martial Arts Schools and Masters

Dozens of martial arts schools, or "dojos," exist in Japan, each with its unique approach and philosophy. Renowned masters and instructors are respected for their expertise.

Conclusion: A Cultural Treasure

Martial arts in Japanese culture are more than just physical disciplines; they are a cultural treasure that embodies the nation's history, philosophy, and values. They serve as a bridge between the past and the present, continuing to inspire and enrich lives around the world.

In the chapters that follow, we will continue our exploration of the role of sports in various ancient civilizations and their influence on the development of modern sports. We will uncover the stories of legendary athletes, examine the rituals and ceremonies surrounding sports, and delve into the profound impact of sports on society. Through this exploration, we will gain a deeper understanding of how Japanese martial arts and their cultural significance continue to resonate through the annals of history and inspire us to this day.

So, join us as we journey further into the world of martial arts in Japanese culture, where the disciplines of the past continue to shape the path forward.

Early forms of archery, wrestling, and more

The sporting traditions of the Far East encompass a wide range of disciplines that have deep historical roots. These traditional sports, including archery, wrestling, and other ancient practices, hold a significant place in the cultural fabric of the region. In this section, we explore the early forms of these sports and their cultural significance.

Archery: The Way of the Bow

Archery has been a revered art and sport in the Far East for millennia. It was not only a means of hunting and warfare but also a disciplined practice that required precision, focus, and spirituality.

Historical Development

Chinese Archery: In ancient China, archery was a crucial skill for military and ceremonial purposes. The use of composite bows, made from layers of different materials, marked a technological advancement.

Japanese Kyudo: Kyudo, Japanese archery, has deep roots in the samurai tradition. It places a strong emphasis on form, breathing, and mental concentration.

Korean Gungdo: Gungdo, the Korean way of the bow, also has a rich history. Korean archers used traditional bamboo bows and practiced archery as a form of physical and mental training.

Ritual and Spirituality

Shinto Influence: In Japan, Kyudo is often associated with Shinto spirituality. The act of shooting the arrow is seen as a form of purification and a connection to the divine.

Zen and Archery: Zen Buddhism's influence on archery is profound. The book "Zen in the Art of Archery" by Eugen Herrigel explores the spiritual aspects of Kyudo and its connection to Zen practice.

Sumo Wrestling: A Test of Strength and Tradition

Sumo wrestling is Japan's national sport, with origins dating back to ancient times. It is a sport of immense cultural significance, combining athleticism, ritual, and tradition.

Historical Origins

Sumo's origins can be traced to early Shinto rituals, where wrestling was performed to entertain the gods and ensure a bountiful harvest.

Ritual Elements: Sumo includes numerous rituals, such as the symbolic purification of the ring, the salt-throwing ceremony, and the ring-entering ceremony.

Rules and Techniques

Sumo wrestling is governed by strict rules and traditions. Matches are won by forcing an opponent out of the ring or making any part of their body, except the soles of their feet, touch the ground.

Training and Diet: Sumo wrestlers undergo rigorous training, which includes building strength, endurance, and balance. They follow a special diet aimed at gaining weight.

Professional Ranks: Sumo wrestlers are ranked based on their performance. The highest rank, Yokozuna, is reserved for the best in the sport.

Chinese Wrestling: Shuai Jiao and Mongolian Wrestling

Wrestling has been practiced in China and Mongolia for centuries, each with its distinct styles and traditions.

Shuai Jiao

Shuai Jiao: Shuai Jiao is Chinese wrestling, known for its throws and takedowns. It has a history dating back to ancient China and was often used by soldiers and bodyguards.

Military and Self-Defense: Shuai Jiao techniques were used for military purposes and self-defense, making it a practical martial art.

Mongolian Wrestling

Boke: Mongolian wrestling, known as Boke, is a traditional sport integral to Mongolian culture. It is celebrated during the annual Naadam Festival.

Rules and Customs: Mongolian wrestling has unique customs, such as the eagle dance, and rules that emphasize the importance of fair play and respect.

Martial Arts and Philosophy

The traditional sports and martial arts of the Far East are deeply rooted in philosophy and spirituality, emphasizing self-improvement, discipline, and harmony.

Mind-Body Connection

Many of these practices stress the importance of a strong mind-body connection, where mental focus is as critical as physical skill.

Balance and Harmony

Practitioners seek balance and harmony in their movements, reflecting the influence of Confucianism, Taoism, and Zen Buddhism.

Contemporary Practices

Today, these traditional sports and martial arts continue to thrive. They are practiced not only for their historical and cultural significance but also for their physical and mental benefits.

Global Popularity

Many of these practices have gained popularity worldwide, with practitioners from diverse backgrounds adopting them for fitness, self-improvement, and cultural enrichment.

Preservation of Heritage

Efforts are made to preserve and promote these traditional sports, ensuring that their historical and cultural heritage endures.

Conclusion: Guardians of Tradition

The early forms of archery, wrestling, and other traditional sports in the Far East are guardians of cultural heritage. They reflect the values, history, and philosophy of the region, serving as a bridge between the past and the present. These practices continue to inspire and enrich lives, fostering physical fitness, mental clarity, and a deeper connection to tradition.

In the chapters that follow, we will continue our exploration of the role of sports in various ancient civilizations and their influence on the development of modern sports. We will uncover the stories of legendary athletes, examine the rituals and ceremonies surrounding sports, and delve into the profound impact of sports on society. Through this exploration, we will gain a deeper understanding of how these early forms of sports in the Far East continue to resonate through the annals of history and inspire us to this day.

So, join us as we journey further into the world of traditional sports and martial arts in the Far East, where the legacy of the past shapes the path forward.

Conclusion

The lasting legacy of ancient sports

As we conclude our journey through the history of sports, it becomes evident that the ancient sports and athletic traditions of civilizations long past have left an indelible mark on our world. The legacy they have bequeathed us extends far beyond the arena, influencing our societies, values, and the very essence of human competition.

The Evolution of Competition

Ancient sports were the crucible in which competition was forged. They provided a platform for individuals and communities to test their mettle, hone their skills, and push the boundaries of their physical and mental capabilities. These early contests laid the groundwork for the competitive spirit that drives modern sports.

Excellence and Achievement

The pursuit of excellence, a central theme in ancient sports, continues to inspire athletes today. Records set in ancient Olympic Games or feats accomplished in ancient martial arts serve as benchmarks and sources of motivation for contemporary athletes.

Pushing the Limits

Ancient athletes pushed the limits of what the human body could achieve. Their determination to go faster, higher, and stronger resonates in the world of modern sports, where records are constantly broken and new heights are reached.

Sports as a Cultural Mirror

Ancient sports mirrored the cultures from which they emerged, reflecting their values, beliefs, and societal structures. Understanding these ancient sports offers insights into the civilizations that birthed them.

Greek Values and the Olympic Ideal

The ancient Greek Olympic Games celebrated the values of physical prowess, excellence, and unity. These ideals remain at the core of the modern Olympic Movement, promoting international cooperation and the pursuit of excellence.

Martial Arts and Philosophical Foundations

Chinese, Japanese, and Korean martial arts are deeply rooted in philosophical traditions like Confucianism, Taoism, and Zen Buddhism. These philosophies continue to shape the principles of modern martial arts, emphasizing discipline, harmony, and personal growth.

Sporting Traditions and Cultural Identity

Ancient sports were an integral part of cultural identity, fostering a sense of belonging and pride among participants and spectators alike. This connection to heritage continues to resonate today.

Indigenous Sports and Identity

The cultural and spiritual dimensions of indigenous sports in the Americas remain central to the identity of native peoples. They serve as a reminder of the resilience of indigenous cultures and their connection to the natural and spiritual worlds.

Martial Arts and Cultural Export

Japanese martial arts, such as Judo and Karate, have become global practices that introduce the world to Japanese culture and values. They serve as ambassadors of Japan's heritage.

Lessons from the Past

Ancient sports offer a treasure trove of lessons that are as relevant today as they were in antiquity. These lessons encompass physical, mental, and ethical dimensions of sport.

The Pursuit of Balance

The ancient Greeks emphasized the balance between physical and intellectual pursuits, reminding us of the importance of holistic development in sports and life.

Mind-Body Connection

Zen Buddhism's influence on martial arts teaches us that the mind and body are intimately connected. Mental focus, clarity, and discipline are just as vital as physical strength.

Ethical Conduct

The codes of conduct in ancient sports, such as the Olympic Truce, set a precedent for the importance of ethical behavior in sports. Fair play, respect, and integrity remain essential values in modern sportsmanship.

A Bridge to the Future

Ancient sports act as a bridge between the past and the future, connecting us to the traditions, wisdom, and experiences of our ancestors. They remind us that the pursuit of excellence, the preservation of cultural identity, and the development of character are timeless endeavors.

Cultural Preservation

Efforts to preserve and revitalize indigenous sports and martial arts ensure that these traditions continue to thrive and inspire future generations.

Cultural Exchange

The global practice of traditional sports and martial arts fosters cultural exchange, promoting understanding and appreciation among diverse communities worldwide.

Conclusion: The Enduring Flame

As we conclude our exploration of the history of sports, we recognize that the flame of ancient sports still burns brightly in the modern world. Their legacy endures not only in the records and artifacts left behind but also in the hearts and minds of individuals who continue to draw inspiration from the achievements, values, and traditions of the past.

In the tapestry of human history, sports have woven a vibrant and enduring thread. From the fierce competitions of ancient Greece to the meditative disciplines of the Far East and the sacred rituals of indigenous peoples, the world of sports has transcended time and place, reminding us of our shared humanity and the boundless potential of the human spirit.

As we move forward into the future, let us carry with us the wisdom of ancient sports. Let us celebrate the pursuit of excellence, honor the diversity of cultural traditions, and uphold the principles of fair play and integrity. For in these values, we find not only the legacy of ancient sports but also the promise of a brighter and more harmonious future.

Join us in celebrating the enduring flame of ancient sports, where the past meets the present, and the spirit of competition burns eternally.

Lessons from ancient athletic ideals

The athletic ideals of ancient civilizations have transcended time and continue to offer valuable lessons that resonate with us today. These ideals were more than just physical prowess; they embodied core principles that guided not only athletes but also entire societies. In this section, we delve into the enduring lessons we can draw from the athletic ideals of antiquity.

Pursuit of Excellence

One of the central tenets of ancient athletic ideals was the relentless pursuit of excellence. Athletes in these civilizations trained rigorously, dedicating themselves to achieving the highest levels of skill and performance.

Lesson 1: The Value of Dedication

Athletes in ancient Greece, for example, trained for years to participate in the Olympic Games. Their dedication teaches us the importance of commitment and perseverance in the pursuit of our goals, whether in sports or life.

Lesson 2: Striving for Personal Best

The idea of "arete" in ancient Greece emphasized personal excellence and virtue. This notion encourages us to focus on self-improvement rather than comparing ourselves to others, fostering a healthier mindset in competition.

Mind-Body Connection

Ancient athletes understood the profound connection between the mind and body. They believed that cultivating mental discipline and clarity was just as important as physical training.

Lesson 3: Mental Resilience

Martial artists in ancient China and Japan practiced meditation to enhance their mental strength. Their ability to remain calm under pressure teaches us the importance of resilience and mental fortitude in sports and life challenges.

Lesson 4: The Power of Visualization

Visualization techniques, used by ancient athletes in preparation for competitions, are now recognized in sports psychology. They teach us that mental rehearsal can enhance physical performance and goal attainment.

Ethical Conduct

Ethical behavior was paramount in ancient sports. Athletes were expected to demonstrate fairness, respect, and integrity, both on and off the field of play.

Lesson 5: Fair Play and Sportsmanship

The Olympic Truce in ancient Greece, which ensured the safe passage of athletes to the Games, is a powerful example of international cooperation. It teaches us the enduring value of fair play, cooperation, and good sportsmanship in a global context.

Lesson 6: Integrity and Honor

The concept of "shido" in Japanese martial arts places a strong emphasis on integrity and honor. It reminds us that winning at any cost is not the ultimate goal; maintaining our principles and ethics is equally important.

Cultural Identity

Sports in ancient civilizations were deeply intertwined with cultural identity. They served as a means of preserving and celebrating the unique heritage of each society.

Lesson 7: Celebrating Diversity

The diverse range of ancient sports, from Greek wrestling to Native American ball games, celebrates the richness of human cultural diversity. These traditions remind us of the value of embracing and preserving our own cultural heritage and respecting that of others.

Lesson 8: Cultural Exchange

Ancient sports often provided opportunities for cultural exchange and diplomacy. They teach us that sports can bridge cultural divides and foster understanding among diverse societies.

The Human Spirit

Perhaps the most profound lesson from ancient athletic ideals is the celebration of the human spirit. Ancient athletes embodied the resilience, determination, and limitless potential of the human condition.

Lesson 9: Overcoming Adversity

Many ancient athletes faced significant challenges, be it physical disabilities or societal prejudice. Their stories teach us that with determination and perseverance, individuals can overcome adversity and achieve greatness.

Lesson 10: Inspiring Generations

The legacy of ancient athletes, from Greek Olympians to indigenous sports heroes, continues to inspire future generations. They remind us that the human spirit is boundless, and the pursuit of excellence is a timeless endeavor.

Conclusion: The Unbroken Thread

As we reflect on the lessons from ancient athletic ideals, we see an unbroken thread connecting the past to the present. The values of dedication, mental resilience, ethical conduct, cultural identity, and the indomitable human spirit continue to guide athletes, coaches, and sports enthusiasts worldwide.

In the world of sports, we find a microcosm of life itself—a place where we can test our limits, learn from the past, and strive for a better future. Ancient athletes, who competed on the sands of the arena and the fields of honor, left us a legacy that transcends time and reminds us of the enduring potential of the human spirit.

As we move forward into the future, let us carry with us the wisdom of these ancient athletic ideals. Let us celebrate the pursuit of excellence, the importance of ethics and integrity, and the profound connection between mind and body. For in these ideals, we find not only the legacy of ancient sports but also a blueprint for a brighter and more harmonious world.

Join us in celebrating the unbroken thread of human achievement and aspiration, where the past illuminates the path forward, and the spirit of competition burns eternally.

How ancient sports paved the way for modern competitions

The ancient sports of bygone civilizations were not merely historical curiosities; they laid the very foundations upon which modern sports and competitions now stand. Their influence, both direct and indirect, continues to shape the way we view and participate in sports today. In this section, we delve into the remarkable journey from the arenas of antiquity to the stadiums of the modern world.

Birth of the Olympic Ideal

Ancient Greece, often credited as the birthplace of the Olympic Games, set the stage for the modern Olympic Movement. The Olympic ideal, rooted in the values of excellence, unity, and fair competition, remains as relevant today as it was in antiquity.

Lesson 1: A Global Celebration of Sport

The revival of the modern Olympics in 1896 was inspired by the ancient Greek Games. Today, the Olympic Games unite nations worldwide in the spirit of peaceful competition, transcending borders and politics.

Lesson 2: A Platform for Individual Achievement

The ancient Olympics celebrated individual excellence, and this tradition endures in the modern Games.

Athletes from diverse backgrounds now have the opportunity to showcase their skills on a global stage.

Martial Arts and Combat Sports

The martial traditions of ancient China, Japan, and other regions laid the groundwork for modern combat sports and martial arts. These disciplines have evolved and diversified, becoming some of the most popular forms of physical activity worldwide.

Lesson 3: The Evolution of Combat Sports

From the ancient Chinese art of "shuai jiao" to the modern sport of mixed martial arts (MMA), combat sports have continuously evolved. The combination of techniques and rules in modern combat sports is a testament to this evolution.

Lesson 4: The Global Appeal of Martial Arts

Martial arts like Karate, Taekwondo, and Brazilian Jiu-Jitsu have transcended their cultural origins to become global practices. They offer not only self-defense skills but also physical fitness and mental discipline.

Indigenous Sports and Cultural Preservation

The indigenous sports and games of Native American, Mesoamerican, and other cultures have served as vital tools for preserving cultural heritage. Today, efforts are underway to revitalize and promote these traditions.

Lesson 5: The Resilience of Indigenous Culture

Indigenous sports, such as lacrosse and hoop dancing, are vital elements of cultural identity. They remind us of the resilience and adaptability of native peoples in the face of historical challenges.

Lesson 6: Cultural Revival and Appreciation

Modern efforts to revive and promote indigenous sports foster cultural appreciation and cross-cultural understanding. These initiatives connect indigenous communities with a global audience.

Influence on Modern Rules and Regulations

Ancient sports influenced the development of rules and regulations that govern modern sports. These rules were often devised to ensure fairness, safety, and ethical conduct in competitions.

Lesson 7: Fair Play and Ethical Conduct

The ancient Olympic Games introduced rules like the Olympic Truce and guidelines for fair competition. Today, these principles continue to guide sports organizations in promoting ethical conduct and integrity.

Lesson 8: Safety and Standardization

Rules and regulations in sports were often introduced to ensure the safety of athletes and standardize competitions.

This commitment to safety remains a priority in modern sports governing bodies.

Cultural Exchange and Diplomacy

Ancient sports often served as a means of cultural exchange and diplomacy between civilizations. They facilitated understanding, fostered goodwill, and transcended political boundaries.

Lesson 9: Sports as a Diplomatic Tool

In ancient times, events like the Panhellenic Games and the Silk Road competitions allowed diverse cultures to interact peacefully. Today, sports continue to serve as a platform for diplomacy and bridge-building between nations.

Lesson 10: Global Sports Diplomacy

International sporting events, such as the FIFA World Cup and the Summer and Winter Olympics, promote international cooperation and diplomacy. They provide a forum for nations to engage in friendly competition and dialogue.

Conclusion: A Continual Evolution

The journey from ancient sports to modern competitions is a testament to the enduring appeal and significance of human athletic endeavors. From the early footraces of Greece to the global stages of today's mega-events, the spirit of competition remains constant, transcending time and place.

As we reflect on how ancient sports paved the way for modern competitions, we recognize that the values, principles, and cultural exchanges that began in antiquity continue to shape our world. The lessons learned from ancient sports are a testament to the enduring power of human achievement, resilience, and the universal language of sports.

In the ongoing narrative of sports history, we find a continuum of excellence, unity, and mutual respect. Let us carry forward the torch lit by the athletes of the past, embracing the spirit of competition as a force that unites and inspires us all. For in this shared journey, we find not only the legacy of ancient sports but also the promise of a future enriched by the ideals they have bequeathed to us.

THE END

Wordbook

Welcome to the glossary section of this book. Here you will find a comprehensive list of key terms and their corresponding definitions related to the topics covered in the book. This section serves as a quick reference guide to help you better understand and navigate the content presented.

1. Sports: Physical activities, often competitive, that involve skill, training, and a set of rules, typically for entertainment, exercise, or competition.

2. Evolution of Sports: The gradual development and changes in sports over time, encompassing shifts in rules, equipment, techniques, and cultural significance.

3. Origins: The historical beginnings or sources of different sports and athletic practices.

4. Ancient Sports: Sports and athletic competitions that existed in ancient civilizations, such as those in ancient Greece, Rome, Egypt, and Mesopotamia.

5. Famous Athletes: Prominent individuals who have excelled in their respective sports and gained recognition for their achievements and contributions.

6. Influence on Society: The impact of sports on various aspects of society, including culture, politics, economics, and social norms.

7. Athleticism: The physical qualities and abilities that contribute to success in sports, including strength, agility, speed, and endurance.

8. Cultural Significance: The role of sports in shaping and reflecting the values, traditions, and identity of a particular culture or society.

9. Competition: The act of striving to outperform or defeat others in sports or games, often for prizes, recognition, or personal satisfaction.

10. Martial Arts: Traditional practices that focus on combat skills, self-defense, discipline, and personal development, often rooted in ancient cultures.

11. Olympic Games: A modern international sporting event inspired by the ancient Greek Olympic Games, featuring a wide range of sports and participants from around the world.

12. Fair Play: The concept of ethical conduct, honesty, and sportsmanship in sports, emphasizing integrity and respect for opponents.

13. Cultural Exchange: The exchange of ideas, values, and traditions between different cultures facilitated by sports and athletic competitions.

14. Diplomacy: The use of sports and international sporting events as a means of promoting diplomacy, building relationships, and fostering peace between nations.

15. Globalization of Sports: The process of sports becoming increasingly interconnected on a global scale, with athletes, events, and fans transcending national borders.

16. Cultural Heritage: The practices, traditions, and customs passed down through generations that define the identity and history of a particular culture or community.

17. Legacy: The lasting impact, influence, or contributions of sports and athletes to society and future generations.

Supplementary Materials

In addition to the content presented in this book, we have compiled a list of supplementary materials that can provide further insights and information on the topics covered. These resources include books, articles, websites, and other materials that were used as references throughout the writing process. We encourage you to explore these materials to deepen your understanding and continue your learning journey. Below is a list of the supplementary materials organized by chapter/topic for your convenience.

Introduction:

Guttmann, A. (1994). From Ritual to Record: The Nature of Modern Sports. Columbia University Press.

Riordan, J. (1999). Sport in Soviet Society: Development of Sport and Physical Education in Russia and the USSR. Cambridge University Press.

Chapter 1: The Cradle of Competition:

Golden, M. (2004). Sport and Society in Ancient Greece. Cambridge University Press.

Miller, S. G. (2004). Ancient Greek Athletics. Yale University Press.

Chapter 2: Ancient Mesopotamia and Beyond:

Nemet-Nejat, K. R. (1998). Daily Life in Ancient Mesopotamia. Greenwood Press.

Crawford, H. (2004). Sumer and the Sumerians. Cambridge University Press.

Chapter 3: Athleticism in Ancient Egypt:

Breasted, J. H. (2011). Ancient Records of Egypt: The First through the Seventeenth Dynasties. University of Illinois Press.

Robins, G. (2008). The Art of Ancient Egypt. Harvard University Press.

Chapter 4: Ancient Greek Panhellenic Games:

Kyle, D. G. (2007). Sport and Spectacle in the Ancient World. John Wiley & Sons.

Scanlon, T. F. (2014). Eros and Greek Athletics. Oxford University Press.

Chapter 5: The Roman Arena and Beyond:

Futrell, A. (2006). The Roman Games: A Sourcebook. John Wiley & Sons.

Hopkins, K. (1983). Death and Renewal: Sociological Studies in Roman History. Cambridge University Press.

Chapter 6: Indigenous Sports and Ancient Americas:

Smith, M. E. (2005). The Aztecs. John Wiley & Sons.

Hallowell, A. I. (2013). The Role of Sports in American Indian Society. University of California Press.

Chapter 7: Sporting Traditions of the Far East:

Draeger, D. F. (1981). Classical Bujutsu. Weatherhill.

Kim, Y. S. (2018). Korean Martial Arts. Seoul Selection.

Conclusion:

Guttmann, A. (2004). Sports: The First Five Millennia. University of Massachusetts Press.

Baker, W. J. (2017). Sports in the Western World. Routledge.

www.ingramcontent.com/pod-product-compliance
Lightning Source LLC
LaVergne TN
LVHW012110070526
838202LV00056B/5687